Welcome

There are so many irresistible plants out there, but how do you ensure that your garden has something to offer throughout the year? Being a self-confessed plantaholic, I often have to pinch myself that I can call on the most knowledgeable nurserymen in the country for their advice and insights. There's nothing quite like working with plants every day to gain the greatest understanding of how a particular plant performs throughout the year and which cultivars and varieties are the best of their kind.

For this special edition, we have gathered together a fine collection of plants chosen by leading experts to give you a wealth of planting ideas from early spring right through to late winter. This thoughtful selection includes well-known garden stalwarts as well as the more unusual, and throughout the emphasis is on easy to grow perennials that will greatly enhance your garden. In addition, you'll find recommendations of the best places to visit to find seasonal inspiration, as well as a shortlist of some of our favourite plant nurseries. I hope you find plenty of ideas and advice to ensure your garden remains lovely throughout the year.

Juliet Roberts, Editor,
Gardens Illustrated magazine

EDITORIAL
Managing Editor Paul McGuinness
Editor Juliet Roberts
Deputy Editor Sorrel Everton
Production Editors Sue Wingrove
& Paul Bloomfield

ART & PICTURES
Art Editor Sheu-Kuei Ho
Picture Editor James Cutmore
Design Tina Smith & Jane Gollner

PRESS AND PUBLIC RELATIONS
Press Officer Carolyn Wray 0117 314 8812
carolyn.wray@immediate.co.uk

CIRCULATION & ADVERTISING
Circulation Manager Rob Brock
Advertising Director Caroline Herbert
Senior Brand Sales Executive Lucy Moakes

PRODUCTION
Production Director Sarah Powell
Production coordinator Emily Mounter
Reprographics Tony Hunt and Chris Sutch

PUBLISHING
Publisher Marie Davies
Publishing Director Andy Healy
Managing Director Andy Marshall
Chairman Stephen Alexander
Deputy Chairman Peter Phippen
CEO Tom Bureau

Contents

Spring

Summer

Plantsmen

DAN PEARSON

Dan is a plantsman and designer, principal of London-based Dan Pearson Studio. Trained at RHS Wisley and the Royal Botanic Gardens at Kew, Dan has was one of the earliest contemporary practitioners of naturalistic perennial planting in the UK. He travels widely to consult and design, and writes a column in *The Observer* magazine.
www.danpearsonstudio.com

GRAHAM GOUGH

Graham is the founder of Marchants Hardy Plants at Laughton in East Sussex. Following a short career in classical music as a tenor, he trained under Elizabeth Strangman at Washfield Nursery in Kent. A respected nurseryman and garden designer, he has also garnered acclaim for his writing and talks about gardening and plant travel.
www.marchantshardyplants.co.uk

FERGUS GARRETT

Fergus is head gardener at Great Dixter in East Sussex, having worked alongside Christopher Lloyd for 15 years. He also lectures, writes and serves on Royal Horticultural Society committees. The nursery at Great Dixter stocks a wide range of interesting, garden-worthy plants, some 80 per cent of them raised on site.
www.greatdixter.co.uk

Where to buy your plants

See page 112 for our directory of great nurseries

Late Summer

Autumn & Winter

CHRIS MARCHANT

Chris is co-owner of Orchard Dene Nurseries in Henley-on-Thames, Oxfordshire, a wholesale grower specialising in hardy herbaceous plants. Orchard Dene works with top British and international garden designers, and is stocked with 1400 varieties carefully chosen for their merits as 'landscape performance plants'.
www.orcharddene.co.uk

JOHN HOYLAND

John is a plantsman, garden writer and owner of Pioneer Nurseries, in the village of Willian on the outskirts of Letchworth, Hertfordshire. With his partner, Nick Downing, John has continued the long tradition of growing beautiful, healthy plants – from the common-or-garden to the rare and the new.
www.pioneerplants.com

BOB BROWN

Bob Brown owns Cotswold Garden Flowers, a magnet for plant lovers, which stocks a huge range of rare and beautiful varieties: good old-fashioned plants; newly introduced plants bred not only for colour and form but also for vigour; and plants newly introduced from the wild.
www.cgf.net

Spring

As longer days and milder weather bring life surging back into your garden, the first precious harbingers of spring unfurl their flowers. Here are some of the loveliest plants to inspire your planting and add zest and colour as the gardening year begins

Saxifraga x *arendsii* 'Pink Carpet'

The mossy dome of this saxifrage has survived for several years in the top of a low shaded wall in my garden. Too much water turns the foliage brown and too much sun will burn it but get the situation right and you are rewarded with a little forest of pink flowers on short, wiry stems.

HEIGHT/SPREAD **10cm x 10cm.**

ORIGINS **Garden hybrid.**

CONDITIONS **Very well-drained soil in part-shade.**

SEASON **April to May.** JH

MAGAZINE SUBSCRIPTION OFFER

SAVE 40%*

when you subscribe to *Gardens Illustrated*

~~£4.99~~
£2.99*
PER ISSUE

SPECIAL SUBSCRIPTION OFFER

● **Save 40% – just £38.92 every 13 issues** by annual Direct Debit*

● **Never miss an issue** of your favourite magazine

● **Free UK delivery** direct to your door

Subscribe online at

buysubscriptions.com/GIP262
or call our subscriber hotline on 03330 162114†

*40% saving is available to UK residents paying by annual Direct Debit only. †UK calls will cost the same as other standard fixed line numbers (starting 01 or 02) and are included as part of any inclusive or free minutes allowances (if offered by your phone tariff). Outside of inclusive or free call packages, call charges from mobile phones will cost between 3p and 55p per minute. Lines are open 8am-6pm, Monday to Friday, and 9am-1pm Saturday. Overseas readers call +44 1604 973 722. You must quote the promotion code given to receive this offer. Offer ends 18 July 2018.

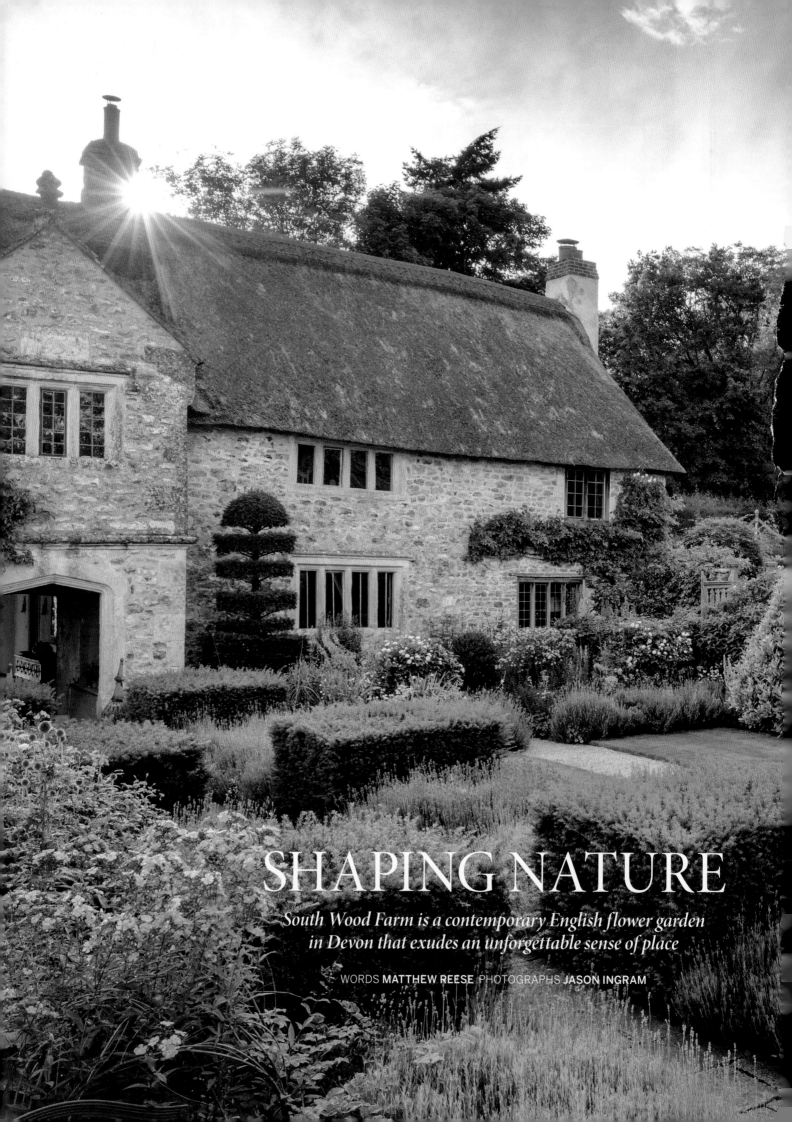

SHAPING NATURE

*South Wood Farm is a contemporary English flower garden
in Devon that exudes an unforgettable sense of place*

WORDS **MATTHEW REESE** PHOTOGRAPHS **JASON INGRAM**

On a south-facing slope, and backed by a shelter belt
of ash and oak, South Wood farmhouse makes
a wonderful focal point for the garden. Here in the
Front Courtyard, the sculptural topiary is a strong
contrast with the mixed border plantings.

MEADOWS FLOW SMOOTHLY THROUGH THE ESTATE FENCING, SOFTENING THE DIVIDE BETWEEN FARMLAND AND GARDEN

At the end of a narrow lane, bordered by overgrown hedgerows that are thick with wildflowers and studded with large English oaks, beech and ash trees, is the ancient homestead of South Wood Farm. Composed of a wonderful collection of chert stone buildings that sit snugly within a pocket of picturesque Devon countryside, South Wood Farm is surrounded by lush, rolling pasture speckled with trees and woodland. The main house, a medieval, cross-passage, yeoman's house (with front and back doors opposite each other and connected via a corridor), dates from the 14th century, with later additions, most notably in 1655 when the house was extended.

South Wood Farm is the country home of Professor Clive Potter, who moved here in 2005. There was little garden here when he arrived so, in 2008, he invited designer Arne Maynard to help lay the foundations for the garden. Clive refurbished the somewhat dilapidated outbuildings and walls that were once part of a dairy farm, while Arne restored the yard from modern concrete to small, chert stone cobbles – the same stone used for the buildings. Chert (a type of flint) is the local stone, and indeed, is often unearthed in the borders; its use in the yard binds the farmhouse and outbuildings to the garden seamlessly. Arne Maynard's skilful incorporation of the old buildings and walls into his design creates a wonderful atmosphere and makes the garden feel much more mature than it is. The garden can be split into four main areas that wrap around the farmhouse: the Driveway, including the yard and meadows; the Front Courtyard, the jewel in the crown of South Wood; the Plum Orchard with its serpentine path; and a productive Kitchen Garden.

One of the most attractive features of the garden is the easy way it sits within the wider landscape. Meadows flow smoothly through the estate fencing, softening the divide between the farmland pasture and garden, and gradually build in intensity as they get closer to the main hub of the garden surrounding the house. Head gardener Will Smithson has been managing the garden with Clive for the past five years. He explains the 'borrowed view' concept by saying "not only does the garden sit comfortably in the landscape, but the landscape is very much part of the garden". Heading towards the Front Courtyard, he stops to point out link plants used to tie the garden to the meadows. *Gladiolus communis* subsp. *byzantinus* and *Athriscus sylvestris* 'Ravenswing' (a type of cow parsley), along with others such as *Astrantia*, *Knautia*, *Deschampsia* and *Molinia*, are used in the borders to echo the meadow flora. Topiary in the garden provides year-round structure and contrasts with the meadows. Will explains that they are beginning to sculpt the hedgerows to create a bond with the topiary and forge a bridge between the more formal aspects of the garden and the wider landscape.

The Front Courtyard is the most intensively managed space in the garden. It sits beneath the beautiful thatched farmhouse, which, as Clive describes it, "glows in the sunshine" and is the perfect foil for the dark yew topiary here. Arne has used a limited palette of roses to give the impression of a frugal farmer who was once given a rose cutting and has gradually increased stock to plant throughout the garden. The colour palette is also limited. "We mainly use pinks, purples and whites, and we repeat combinations through the borders," says Will. The garden begins in spring with tulips, and continues with alliums and annuals, through to perennials and roses in midsummer. Climbing roses are planted against the outer walls, with *Rosa* 'Climbing Cécile Brünner' expertly trained along the south-facing wall, and one of Clive's favourites, *R.* 'Cooperi' (Cooper's Burmese), on the house. "I love its simplicity," he says, although Will adds that "it's a thug to prune".

To the north, a sunken, serpentine path draws you up from the Front Courtyard through a meadow to the Plum Orchard. Here nine plum trees (three each of three varieties) are laid out across a square. Each is underplanted with beech clipped into a plinth-like square. Beyond these are two elegant oak benches (commissioned from Arne) that look back towards the house and are planted on either side ▷

Above View from the Front Courtyard along the York path into the cross-passage corridor that connects the oldest 14th-century part of the house to the later extension carried out in 1655. The espalier crab apples connect the house with the outbuildings, and enclose the courtyard.

Below The planting in the Front Courtyard is a mixed affair, with small swathes of perennials, and roses trained on hazel hoops repeated through the borders. The limited pallete its a take on the frugal yeoman who might have built his garden with cuttings gleaned from friends and by repeating his favourites.

Above The clipped bay, planted by the previous owners in 1998, was retained and reshaped into a cone and now forms a focal point in the Front Courtyard garden. Four paths divide the garden into sections. The lavender that edges the beds has since been replaced with brick edging.

Below Brick steps lead to the Kitchen Garden. The pretty oak gate set into one of the original chert walls is a good example of Arne's attention to detail. The use of oak creates a direct link between the house and the garden, making the house sit more comfortably with the garden and vice versa.

Above Head gardener Will Smithson pays particular attention to the roses, all of which are fastidiously trained. In the borders he attaches them to a skeleton of hazel. It is important to stake them carefully, as the area is subject to high winds.

Below At the base of the south-facing chert wall, *Stipa gigantea* and *Verbena bonariensis* combine with self-sowers *Linaria purpurea* 'Canon Went' and *Verbascum blattaria* f. *albiflorum* in airy displays. The hornbeam topiary is a nice full-stop at the end of the border, the curved top echoing the large oaks.

Above Understanding the importance of proportions and balance when designing a garden is crucial so that garden and house sit comfortably together. Here, looking across the Kitchen Garden, there is complete harmony between the two.

Below Espalier fruit, meadows, a chert cobble path and wooden pillars give way to the more formal plantings. This buffer zone eases the transition from the informal meadows to the more formal Front Courtyard garden. Will uses flowering garden plants that have a meadow feel to help soften the change.

View of the Plum Orchard, looking towards the serpentine path and meadow. Each plum tree is planted with a beech plinth. The orchard makes a nice shady contrast to the lighter more open spaces in the garden. Trained fruit trees are one of Arne's trademarks, as they are a flexible way to form permanent structure, particularly in a vegetable garden. They can be used to create entrances, divisions of allées, or to punctuate spaces, and they take up very little ground space. Here the tracery of their branches form a transparent screen in front of the buildings behind.

INCORPORATING OLD WALLS INTO THE DESIGN MAKES THE GARDEN FEEL MORE MATURE

▷ with *Rosa spinosissima* (burnet rose) and *Geranium macrorrhizum* 'White Ness'. Next to the orchard is the Kitchen Garden, which, judging by the plant labels Will has dug up, has always been used as such. Arne used lawn paths to divide the space into four squares, each subdivided into smaller plots with step-over pears and raised beds framed with oak boards. Produce and cut flowers are grown for the house; sweet peas, a favourite of Clive's, are always included. Will favours the organic, no-dig method, citing a reduction in weeds as one of the main benefits. The Kitchen Garden is also home to a sunken glasshouse used to propagate and grow plants for the garden at large.

The garden continues to grow since Arne laid it out. There is a new parterre behind the house, a nuttery, and, beneath a copse, a circular pond that is in the throes of being planted. Clive and Will have taken a quality design, a beautiful house and a stunning English landscape, and created a superb and elegant garden in a very little time. □

USEFUL INFORMATION
Address Cotleigh, Honiton, Devon EX14 9HU. **Open** By prior arrangement from 22 May to 30 September 2018, email williamjamessmithson@gmail.com for details.
Find out more about Arne Maynard's work at **arnemaynard.com**

Turn the page for 16 key plants.

16 KEY PLANTS

1 Verbascum blattaria f. albiflorum
This beautiful white-flowered moth mullein is a light, airy biennial that will happily self-sow on lighter soils, and looks great woven through perennial plantings. 1.8m. RHS H6†.

2 Papaver rhoeas
The corn poppy is a wonderful opportunist that will find its way from the border into paving and gravel paths – best grown on poor soils to keep it stocky and upright. 75cm. RHS H7, USDA 3a-10b.

3 Ammi majus
Can be grown as either an annual or biennial. Sown in late summer, it will make huge mounds of white, lacy flowers atop bushy, branching plants. 90cm. AGM*. RHS H6.

4 Lathyrus odoratus Royal Navy Blue
A good, dark-purple-blue sweet pea from the Royal series, which has larger flowers and more blooms than the Spencer type. 2m. RHS H3.

5 Allium sphaerocephalon
A tough perennial onion with small, tight, purple flowers on thin, strong stems. Good with grasses. 50cm. AGM. RHS H6, USDA 4a-8b.

6 Angelica sylvestris 'Vicar's Mead'
A tall, slender biennial or short-lived perennial that can self-sow. Weave through the border or place at the back. 2m. RHS H6.

7 Verbena bonariensis
A tall, wiry, short-lived perennial or annual with little foliage and thin green stems. It makes an excellent see-through plant for the border. 2m. AGM. RHS H4, USDA 7a-11.

8 Stachys byzantina
The soft grey foliage of this herbaceous perennial is a good foil for stronger colours in the border, and looks particularly good with this hardy Salvia verticillata 'Purple Rain'. 50cm. RHS H7, USDA 4a-8b.

Galanthus 'S. Arnott'

Not the rarest or most unusual snowdrop but for me the best – and it holds an Award of Garden Merit from the RHS. Neat, lengthy, grey-green leaves support tall slender stalks of heavy, globular, nodding flowers. With the slightest hint of winter sun the broadly cupped outer sepals lift up like helicopter blades, revealing elegantly held inner petals distinctly marked in arches of green. Clean and crisp, and delicately scented, 'S. Arnott' never fails to bring winter alive. Bulbs increase at the drop of a hat and clumps looks great rising up among a sea of mauve *Crocus tommasinianus.*

HEIGHT/SPREAD **20cm.** AGM.*

ORIGINS **Bred in the 1800s by Samuel Arnott.**

CONDITIONS **Sun or part shade, good soil, moist but well-drained alkaline soil.**

SEASON **Flower February to March. FG**

SHARON PEARSON

Prunus x yedoensis

A garden hybrid known only since 1868, the Tokyo cherry takes its name from Japan's capital, where it has been so generously planted. Among the first cherries to enthral us in spring, the clusters of single saucer-shaped flowers erupt from pink buds in profusion on naked branches – a vision in blush pink and issuing a strong almond scent. The starry sepals and crimson stamens enhance the aging flower with a distinct eye. Elegant in profile and easily pleased, this small tree exits in an autumn blaze of fiery reds and oranges.

HEIGHT/SPREAD 15m x 10m.
ORIGINS Japan.
CONDITIONS Likes moderately fertile, moist but well-drained soil.
SEASON Pale pink flowers in spring, small red fruits and vibrant autumn foliage. **GG**

THANKS TO GREAT DIXTER WWW.GREATDIXTER.CO.UK

SHARON PEARSON

Narcissus tazetta

A highly variable species daffodil found from southern Europe to China. Handsome, long, dark green leaves are early to emerge in December followed later by powerfully scented flowers in February. Each stem carries an umbel of up to 15 small flowers with broad creamy white petals and a short pale yellow corona. Cultivars such as 'Paperwhite', 'Grand Soleil' and 'Ziva' are more popular in cultivation but in my eyes the species has an unrivalled elegance. Planted with *Eucomis*, one bulb takes after another for a seamless succession.

HEIGHT/SPREAD 50cm. AGM.
ORIGINS Southern Europe through to China.
CONDITIONS Best in good, rich soil. Prefers a warm sunny corner.
SEASON End of January to March. **FG**

"With the slightest hint of winter sun the broadly cupped outer sepals lift up like helicopter blades, revealing elegantly held inner petals distinctly marked in arches of green"

Galanthus 'S. Arnott'

Narcissus 'Baby Moon'

The grass-like foliage of this miniature daffodil makes it one of the best to naturalise in short grass: as the leaves die down they don't jar with the surrounding grass. The sweetly scented flowers, with neatly rounded petals, are simple and charming. It is the sort of flower a child draws. Plant as many as you have space for and divide the clumps every three or four years. Grow a few in pots to keep near the house so that you can enjoy the scent on those days when you don't feel brave enough to venture out.

HEIGHT/SPREAD 15cm x 5cm.
ORIGINS This cultivar was bred in the Netherlands in the 1950s.
CONDITIONS Well-drained soil is essential.
SEASON March to April. **JH**

RACHEL WARNE

RACHEL WARNE

Fritillaria meleagris var. unicolor subvar. alba

The snake's head fritillary is a frustrating plant. For those whose gardens meet its specific conditions it will produce masses of healthy seedlings; plant them in less than ideal conditions and you will watch them dwindle and die. There are no half-measures: if you don't have cool, damp soil (ideally a flood meadow) you can't grow it. But what a joy when the plant is happy! *F. meleagris* has dark purple flowers but is at its best when planted with the diaphanous white form. Each benefits from the other and together they sparkle.

HEIGHT/SPREAD 25cm x 5cm. AGM.
ORIGINS Continental Europe, southern UK.
CONDITIONS Soil that stays cool and damp in spring but dries out during the summer.
SEASON March to April. **JH**

Tulipa 'Cairo'

I could fill this whole page with exhortations to grow more tulips. With the fickleness common to most gardeners the list of my favourite tulips is constantly changing. This one has been on the list since I first came across it a few years ago. The flowers have the shallow bowl shape of English florists' tulips and the orange petals are suffused with bronze. It is the result of a long breeding programme that came to fruition in the Netherlands in the 1990s. The sight of a group of them backlit by the low April sunshine will make you catch your breath.

HEIGHT/SPREAD 40cm x 10cm.
ORIGINS Bred in the Netherlands.
CONDITIONS Well-drained fertile soil, or grow in pots.
SEASON April to May. **JH**

RACHEL WARNE

Places to visit

John Hoyland recommends places to visit for a good display of plants in spring

Fritillaria meadows are becoming rare in Britain. One of the best is at **Magdalen College, Oxford**. Bounded on all sides by the River Cherwell, the meadow is maintained to provide the best conditions for *F. meleagris* and is viewed from Addison's Walk, which runs around the meadow.

At **Anglesey Abbey** the tradition of bedding out hundreds of hyacinths, begun

Magdalen College meadow, Oxford

JONATHAN BUCKLEY / GAP PHOTOS

in the early part of last century by Lord Fairhaven, is carried on by the National Trust. The planting is formal, regimented and stunning. Anglesey Abbey, Gardens and Lode Mill, Quy Road, Lode, Cambridge, Cambridgeshire CB25 9EJ. Tel 01223 810080, www.nationaltrust.org.uk

A short drive away, near Bottisham Lock, near Cambridge, is a **National**

Muscari armeniacum 'Valerie Finnis'

The late Valerie Finnis was a knowledgeable plantswoman who was generous in giving away plants. When a nurseryman spotted this in her garden she insisted he took a piece. He named it after her and, thanks to micro-propagation, it is widely available. It is the most beautiful muscari, with pale green buds that open to delicate baby-blue flowers, when the whole plant looks like a piece of Chinese porcelain. Because the flowers are sterile, the plant can only spread by bulb offsets, so it won't overrun your garden.

HEIGHT/SPREAD 20cm x 5cm, spreading.
ORIGINS Eastern Mediterranean species.
CONDITIONS Needs well-drained soil and prefers a sunny spot but will grow in shade.
SEASON March to April. **JH**

RACHEL WARNE

RACHEL WARNE

Hyacinthus orientalis 'L' Innocence'

Most hyacinths have suffered the ignominy of being take out of the garden and put into the forcing shed to become interior decorations. In the garden they are easy, trouble-free bulbs and even a small group will fill the slightest breeze with scent. The luminescent flowers of this cultivar brighten the grey days of March. After a few years the stems are never as packed with flowers as those on supermarket shelves, but the looser, relaxed appearance makes the plant a more comfortable companion to early flowering perennials.

HEIGHT/SPREAD 25cm x 10cm. AGM.
ORIGINS An old garden hybrid. The species grows in western Asia.
CONDITIONS Well-drained soil and full sun.
SEASON March to April. **JH**

Trillium kurabayashii

This is an unusual-looking plant, yet its exotic aura melds superbly in the woodland garden. Known as the wake robin, it is said to emerge when robins become active. In partial shade, and deep, leafy loam, the tubers will be reminded enough of their native Californian/Oregon habitat to produce a crop of dramatic, stalkless and erect, wing-like flowers in polished purple, perched on bold leaves splashed like combat gear camouflage. Structurally arranged in threes (hence their Latin name), a long-established clump will, like the Holy Trinity, be much revered.

HEIGHT/SPREAD 35cm x 20cm. AGM.
ORIGINS Western USA.
CONDITIONS Moist, deep, humus-rich, leafy loam, well drained.
SEASON Maroon flowers in spring, from striking foliage. **GG**

SHARON PEARSON

Collection of hyacinths. Follow Sat Nav CB25 9QL then look for the hyacinth signs – you smell the blooms, grown in a two-acre field, well before you see them. The collection is open, for a small charge, the last weekend of March each year. Check before your visit by emailing alan.shipp@virgin.net or calling 01223 571064.

To get ideas about how to use bulbs, head for Somerset and **Christine Skelmersdale's Broadleigh Gardens.** Familiar as the owner of Broadleigh Bulbs, her display garden is a beautiful showcase for the bulbs she sells. Bishops Hull, Taunton, Somerset TA4 1AE. Open most weekdays. Tel 01823 286231, www.broadleighbulbs.co.uk **Batsford Arboretum** in Gloucestershire contains one of Britain's largest private

Batsford Arboretum

MARTIN PAGE / GETTY

collections of trees and shrubs. In March you can stroll beneath flowering Japanese cherry trees and magnolias which are enhanced by pools of spring-flowering bulbs and wild spring flowers. Batsford Park, Moreton-in-Marsh, Gloucestershire GL56 9AB. Open most days. Tel 01386 701441, www.batsarb.co.uk

Epimedium grandiflorum 'Wildside Red'

Barrenwort's many medicinal uses include a cure for impotency. The Chinese confidently name it horny goat weed – small wonder this beautiful genus encourages a bounce in one's spring stride. From Asia and Europe, and related to *Berberis*, these woodland perennials are sustained by a woody crown and a matrix of wiry roots, their delicate looks belying their toughness. This is a long-spurred crimson selection of *E. grandiflorum*, a Japanese species.

HEIGHT/SPREAD 30cm x 30cm. AGM.
ORIGINS Eastern Asia.
CONDITIONS Fertile, moist, humus rich and well drained.
SEASON The plant has large blooms in mid to late spring. **GG**

SHARON PEARSON

JASON INGRAM

Corylopsis pauciflora

I first noticed this plant in Windsor Great Park, where Eric Savill had set it among hydrangeas to give stoic winter visitors a visual prize. The name suggests a 'shortage' of flowers, but in reality the small clusters of butter-yellow blooms are grouped rather generously along dark, slender stems. Deliciously scented, they cut well and make a delightful airy display for the house – particularly when grouped with brightly coloured willow stems. The appeal continues through delicate hazel-like foliage, margined rosy purple on opening. In autumn the leaves take on warmer tints to give a final glowing salute before falling.

HEIGHT/SPREAD Eventually 2m x 2m. AGM.
ORIGINS Native of Taiwan and Japan.
CONDITIONS Moist, humus-rich soil.
SEASON Flowers February to March with interesting autumn foliage. **CM**

Chaenomeles speciosa 'Yukigotan'

The ornamental 'quinces' are some of the most beautiful of early flowering shrubs, either free-standing or trained against a sheltered wall. Saucer-shaped semi-double flowers are held in dense clusters, outlasting the single forms. They are a curious limey green shade in bud and when freshly unfurled, they mature to a pure white, the snowy starkness of the flowers offset by golden stamens. The effect is dramatic when shown against a dark woodland-mulched soil. Prune back last year's growth after flowering in late spring to maintain shape.

HEIGHT/SPREAD **1.5m x 2m.**
ORIGINS **Japanese cultivar.**
CONDITIONS **Most fertile, well-drained soils, including clay.**
SEASON **Flowers in February, fruit in June-July. CM**

TIM GAINEY / ALAMY

"Pendulous flowering racemes, like oversized drop earrings, adorn burnished mahogany stems, as yet unclothed by leaves"

Stachyurus praecox

Narcissus 'Jack Snipe'

Not a rare thing at all, but nonetheless valuable for that. This diminutive and jaunty plant is a hybrid of *N. cyclamineus*, from which it has inherited the same hardiness. 'Jack Snipe', developed by hybridiser MP Williams in 1951, naturalises beautifully in our garden, on grassy banks at the base of a stand of birches. Slightly reflexed outer petals and a longer trumpet give the happy impression that the stems are leaning into the breeze and the colour counter-balance is easy on the eye.

HEIGHT/SPREAD 25cm x 10cm. AGM.
ORIGINS Hybrid whose parents include native Portuguese species *N. cyclamineus*.
CONDITIONS Moderately fertile, well-drained soil. Application of tomato fertiliser in early spring will increase flowering.
SEASON Late February to March. **CM**

Hepatica transsilvanica

A name derived from the Greek *hepar*, meaning liver. Early herbalists thought the plant held medicinal benefit for ailments of the liver on the basis that its leaves resembled a liver in their three-lobed formation. Medicine has come a long way since then. Now the plant is valued for its ornamental qualities. Moist soil and winter snowfall are the catalyst to a good display. One of the season's early treasures, we have them in a raised stone sink at the threshold from house to garden, where daily encounter ensures we don't miss their moment of radiance.

HEIGHT/SPREAD 15cm x 18cm. AGM.
ORIGINS The Carpathian Mountains, Eastern Europe.
CONDITIONS Tolerates a range of soils from sandy to clay, including alkaline soils.
SEASON February to early March. **CM**

Helleborus x hybridus 'Yellow Lady'

There are so many beautiful hellebores that I can't choose just one as a favourite, but this deserves a mention. Usually unmarked, the flowers are occasionally speckled burgundy at the base of the nectaries. Upright stems hold the flowers proud of the foliage, giving a perfect opportunity to appreciate their long-lasting display. The colour is especially effective teamed with the purples and blues of a woodland border: I have clumps of them mixed with *Pulmonaria* 'Blue Ensign' and the glossy spring foliage of giant colchicums.

HEIGHT/SPREAD 45cm x 35cm.
ORIGINS Developed by German breeder Gisela Schmiemann.
CONDITIONS Humus-rich, moisture-retentive soil.
SEASON February to April. **CM**

Places to visit

Chris Marchant shares some of her favourite gardens and other places to see plants at their best

Early Spring is the perfect opportunity to see some of this country's magnificent parkland plantings at their naked best. Devoid of leaves, the real sculptural beauty of established trees is heightened; undulating contours of the landscape are more evident – even more so with a sharp hoar frost or dusting of snow. One such favourite is **Blenheim Estate**,

Stately trees in a late fall of snow at the Blenheim Estate in Oxfordshire

surrounding the superb baroque architecture of Blenheim Palace. Currently home to the 11th Duke and Duchess of Marlborough, this was the birthplace of Sir Winston Churchill whose father Lord Randolph Churchill described the Vanbrugh Bridge and imposing rides up to the Column of Victory as 'the finest view in England'. It

Ribes laurifolium 'Rosemoor'

This shrub is slow to establish, and you may have to wait a couple of seasons for your first flowers, but patience is a virtue and you will be rewarded. When trained against a sheltered, sunny wall, the dark green, leathery leaves are protected from icy winds that might otherwise scorch the margins. Red stalks, supporting pendulous bunches of flowers, form exciting dashes of colour across the plant and are a perfect lift to its understated elegance. It generously produces shiny black berries later in the season for a final encore.
HEIGHT/SPREAD 1–2m x 2m.
ORIGINS China.
CONDITIONS Most soils including heavy clay. Sheltered spot.
SEASON Flowers in February, with berries in spring. **CM**

Stachyurus praecox

As we emerge from the gloomy greys of winter I am drawn to the elegant simplicity of this shrub. Pendulous flowering racemes, like oversized drop earrings, adorn burnished mahogany stems, as yet unclothed by leaves. Spring brings many bright yellow flowers, but these are of softer, creamy hue and marry well with the many emerging greens at this time. Viewed from a distance, the branches gently arch under the sheer weight of their flowery load.
HEIGHT/SPREAD 3m x 4m. AGM.
ORIGINS South Hokkaido, Japan.
CONDITIONS Easily grown in moist woodland soil in part shade.
SEASON February to March. **CM**

Chionodoxa forbesii 'Alba'

Glory of the snow is native to Western Turkey, where it grows on stony hillsides, flowering as the snow melts. The still, cool days of early spring are a time for stooping low to catch the detailed perfection of smaller flowering bulbs, and there are none more deserving of our attention than these. I have planted them in drifts, nestled between the protective foliage of bolder subjects like *Cyclamen* and small-leaved bergenias. They are best grown through a coarse, dry, gritty mulch to stop rain-splash spoiling their perfect white attire.
HEIGHT/SPREAD 15cm x 15cm.
ORIGINS Western Turkey.
CONDITIONS Stony, free-draining soil.
SEASON February to March. **CM**

would be a brave man who argued against such claims and continuing investment ensures standards are not slipping. Water Terraces, Rose Gardens and Formal Garden all re-open mid February after winter closure. Woodstock, Oxfordshire OX20 1PP. Open most months of the year. Tel 01993 810 530, www.blenheimpalace.com

For a totally different winter scene, **The Valley Gardens**, on the north shore of the large lake Virginia Water in Windsor Great Park, laid out by Eric Savill, demonstrate in confident fashion the colour and textural range of ericaceous (calcifuge) woodland landscape on a grand scale. There are plenty of trails and pathways to explore through the 250

The woodland landscape of The Valley Gardens

acres. The Valley Gardens are open access and easily approached from the car park (there's a charge for parking) of the nearby Savill Gardens which has a good shop as well as a restaurant to complete the day. Savill Gardens, near Englefield Green, Egham, Surrey TW20 0UU. Tel 01784 435544, www.theroyallandscape.co.uk

Prunus mume 'Beni-chidori'

I first saw this at Hyde Hall in Essex on a winter visit in 1982 and it took me 20 years
to find one to buy. It has button-like flowers of rich rose-madder, which are unusually
deeply coloured for a winter bloomer. The flowers are borne on glossy, green, twiggy
shoots (described in The Times as 'pleasingly arthritic'). They are nicely fragrant.
Although it is a form of Japanese apricot, I've not had fruits yet.

HEIGHT/SPREAD **2–3m, shrubby.**

ORIGINS **Korea, Northern China and Japan. This is a Japanese selection.**

CONDITIONS **Most garden conditions. Shelter is not necessary for the flowers.**

SEASON **Flowers in mid to late winter. BB**

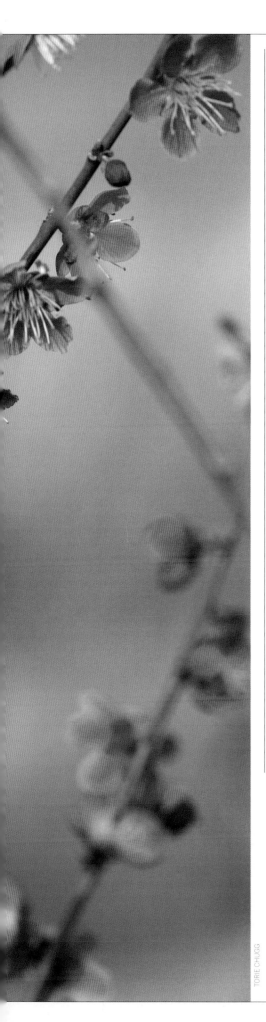

Scilla mischtschenkoana 'Tubergeniana'

Mi-shenk-oh-ana (or something like that) is easier to say than spell. I've had a slowly expanding patch in awful clay soil for nearly 20 years. In January the first flowers appear at ground level and get spattered with mud but by February the flowers are taller, beyond the spatter zone. Utterly wonderful and cooperative, it won't spread too much. Its flowers are lovely and would attract attention in any season.

HEIGHT/SPREAD 15 x 15cm. AGM.
ORIGINS Russia.
CONDITIONS Anywhere except under evergreens. Plant it among a durable herbaceous perennial such as Michaelmas daisies, so you won't dig it up by mistake.
SEASON Mid to late winter. **BB**

Galanthus 'Desdemona'

I love snowdrops, but not for the minutiae of markings that distinguish one cultivar from another. To me, the important differences are season of flowering, quality of the foliage, whether they are single or double and the flower size. 'Desdemona' is a large double – a superb, even-petalled large double – and double snowdrops (unlike single forms) hardly close their flowers when the weather is bad. This means that it has a more persistent effect in the garden. It's also vigorous and quickly increases to fill a space.

HEIGHT/SPREAD 18 x 10cm.
ORIGINS Selected by snowdrop grower Heyrick Greatorex in Norfolk.
CONDITIONS Anywhere – under trees, shrubs and herbaceous perennials or in grass.
SEASON Flowers mid to late winter. **BB**

"The commonest form of crocus has lovely pale silvery lilac flowers. 'Roseus' is a more conspicuous colour, but this rich, pure, pale red softened with grey on the outside is utterly exquisite"

Crocus tommasinianus 'Roseus'

Cardamine quinquefolia

This is one of those really accommodating plants that self-seeds and runs around and *never* causes problems. Viewed close-up, the flowers might be considered weedy but en masse they are wonderful. It has early, deep mauve-pink flowers between February and May when they disappear and become dormant during summer. This plant is vigorous, tolerant, effective and goes to bed early, letting other plants grow through it. Like many invasive plants you need to plant the first one. Buy it.

HEIGHT/SPREAD 12 x 20cm.
ORIGINS Eastern Europe and Western Asia.
CONDITIONS Plant it everywhere; under trees, among shrubs and in herbaceous borders.
SEASON Late winter and spring. **BB**

Echeveria rosea

A succulent that has been grown in Britain since 1841. Until now it has been thought to be tender. It isn't, at least to -12°C. Frankly, it's dull unless grown *outside*, where stress caused by the cold brings a rich red colour to both leaves and the thick spikes of stunning flowers. If you have one inside, though, don't move it outside suddenly in the winter – it should experience increments of cold slowly. Plant it in summer and let it acclimatise gradually. The best planting I know is in a shallow, architectural vase, where it bleeds over the sides all winter.

HEIGHT/SPREAD 12 x 40cm.
ORIGINS Mexico.
CONDITIONS Shallow planters, hot dry sites with plants that won't overwhelm it.
SEASON Foliage December to May, flowers February to May. **BB**

Corydalis solida 'Beth Evans'

Colours other than yellow and blue are welcome in February. This has scented pink flowers until April. I used to have a patch until it succumbed to an accident (involving a spade – in summer). Next time I'll plant it among something that will grow though it (and defend it when it's dormant). Beth was the wife of Alf Evans (1920-2001), assistant curator of the Royal Botanic Garden in Edinburgh, from whence it probably came. The foliage is feathery and grey-green and quickly dissolves as the plant goes dormant at the end of April.

HEIGHT/SPREAD 12 x 10cm.
ORIGINS Most of Europe; Western Asia.
CONDITIONS Grows anywhere (even under trees) unless it gets waterlogged.
SEASON Late winter to early spring. **BB**

Places to visit

Bob Brown suggests gardens to visit that are at their best in early spring

Intimate gardens with winter interest tend to be very special. Their owners are plantswomen (or men) of the first order. Margaret Owen has created one at **The Patch**, Acton Pigot, Shropshire SY5 7PH. She usually has an open day for snowdrops in February but the garden is alive with other attractions. Check for open days at www.opengardens.co.uk

Dial Park

Olive Mason's garden **Dial Park** is a special garden at any time but winter is a particularly important season. If you visit, observe the quiescent plants that will make this a very special garden in successive seasons. Chaddesley Corbett, Worcestershire DY10 4QB. Opens in aid of the National Gardens Scheme. www.ngs.org.uk

Anemone blanda
'Ingramii CE&H 626'

A. blanda is a star – so easy, persistent and cheering on cold late winter and early spring days. I buy them by the thousand in October and broadcast them to grow in deepest dry shade under deciduous trees. I cover them with soil – often obtained from other places – and they pull themselves down. 'Ingramii CE&H 626' has exquisite (and unusual), dark blue, starry flowers over purplish foliage and is much earlier and longer-flowering than other kinds. Wonderful and vigorous.

HEIGHT/SPREAD 12 x 12cm.

ORIGINS This cultivar was collected on Mount Parnassus in Southern Greece.

CONDITIONS Plant somewhere that dries out in summer; say, under a deciduous tree.

SEASON Late winter and spring. **BB**

Crocus tommasinianus
'Roseus'

Few crocuses self-seed in British gardens. If they persist at all, they only clump-up as the corms multiply. *Crocus tommasinianus* can self-seed to cover a garden given enough time and the right neutral, heavy loam soil. The commonest form has lovely pale silvery lilac flowers that close in cold weather into invisible pencil-slim shapes. 'Roseus' is fatter when closed and a more conspicuous colour. This rich, pure, pale red softened with grey on the outside is utterly exquisite for about two weeks some time in late winter.

HEIGHT/SPREAD 15 x 4cm.

ORIGINS Balkans.

CONDITIONS Plant where it avoids summer wet; neutral, heavy loam soil.

SEASON Flowers in late winter. **BB**

Ribes laurifolium
'Mrs Amy Doncaster'

Beekeepers and *Ribes laurifolium* growers realise that honeybees fly all winter (in half decent weather). The flowers smell of sugar water so I presume are a rich source of nectar. This cultivar bears male flowers and smaller, female ones. It's reckoned to be a better-shaped plant than the species, being less sprawly, but mine is tightly tied-in on a wall under a window, so I wouldn't know. It's suitable there because it doesn't get very high. It has nice evergreen foliage. Why do so many green-flowered plants bloom in winter?

HEIGHT/SPREAD 1.3m, shrubby.

ORIGINS China.

CONDITIONS Grows anywhere; train on walls or prune to shape in open borders.

SEASON Mid to late winter. **BB**

Most visitors make it to **Tresco Abbey Gardens** in summer. I am assured (and I believe it) that the most interesting time to visit is midwinter, if you can get there. Sadly I have yet to go. Tresco, Isles of Scilly, Cornwall TR24 0QQ. Open most days. Tel 01720 424108, www.tresco.co.uk

Winter visits to **RHS Hyde Hall** were part of my conversion to growing plants for winter interest. Helen Robinson worked wonders for even January visits (helped, I suppose, by the drier climate in Essex) and provided soup and cake as backup. Creephedge Lane, Rettendon, Chelmsford, Essex CM3 8ET. Open most days. www.rhs.org.uk/gardens

The **Old Vicarage at East Ruston** is a wonderful venue

RHS Hyde Hall

for all kinds of plants. It lies 1½ miles from the North Sea in an exposed prairie landscape but the garden been planted with shelter belts to create unique microclimates that harbour many rare and unusual plants. East Ruston, Norwich, Norfolk NR12 9HN. Seasonal opening. Tel 01692 650432, www.e-ruston-oldvicaragegardens.co.uk

Veratrum nigrum

Veratrum nigrum's broad-arching, pleated foliage is poisonous, but who goes around eating foliage, apart from snails? For me the maroon-black flowers, in July and August, are its *secondary* attraction. If you want to buy this, expect to pay a lot of money – it takes about ten years from seed to make a decent plant. Having said that, it has self-seeded for me – which made me feel I'd finally made it as a gardener. It can be divided in late autumn or early winter, but most owners cherish it too much to disturb it.

HEIGHT/SPREAD Leaves 50 x 50cm, flowers 1-2m tall. AGM.
ORIGINS Central Europe to Korea and China.
CONDITIONS Shade/half-shade, but not too dry.
SEASON Late winter to late summer. **BB**

Fritillaria sinica
pink speckled form

The attraction is twofold. Firstly, it flowers early for a fritillary. Secondly, the colour is not khaki or green or brown (like most other known fritillaries) but crimson speckled with white and pink. The native snake's head fritillary, *F. meleagris*, grows best for me under deciduous trees that dry the soil out in summer. I have yet to plant this beauty out but when I do it will go into similar conditions. Thus far I grow it in pots in loam compost (not peat, which retains too much moisture).

HEIGHT/SPREAD 30 x 10cm.
ORIGINS Native to China.
CONDITIONS Grow in pots or under deciduous trees.
SEASON Flowers in early spring. **BB**

Clematis armandii 'Apple Blossom'

The normal advice is to give this a sunny wall. I think it grows better on a sunless north wall where the foliage doesn't burn – from desiccating winter winds, bad frosts or too much sun. The dramatic three-veined, glossy, dark, evergreen leaves are at least as important as the heavy clusters of scented apple blossom-coloured flowers in early spring. This is a vigorous climber and you (or more likely your spouse/partner) need mental preparation for its rapid spread. Grow it up secure wires running across a house wall (make sure the soffits will not allow ingress), up trees you don't care about too much or over arbours shielding compost heaps.

HEIGHT/SPREAD **Evergreen climber 5 x 3m.** AGM.
ORIGINS **China.**
CONDITIONS **It prefers rich soils, moisture and shelter but is fairly accommodating.**
SEASON **Foliage all the year, flowers in early spring.** BB

"The dramatic three-veined, glossy, dark, evergreen leaves are at least as important as the heavy clusters of scented apple blossom-coloured flowers in early spring"

Clematis armandii 'Apple Blossom'

Scilla messeniaca (MS 38)

Every year I'm surprised by how effective, hardy, well behaved and easy this is. I expect plants from alpine nurseries to need cosseting. Far from it. Mine is planted in what has become a thick row in clay soil next to the ditch and the dense stripe of blue makes visitors abandon the path to find out what it is. It bears large heads of 7–15 blue flowers from February to April. My clone is from a specimen found in Greece by Mike Salmon of Monocot Nursery in Somerset, hence the 'MS 38' collection number above. A superb, long-lived plant.

HEIGHT/SPREAD 15 x 15cm.
ORIGINS Greece.
CONDITIONS Anywhere, but not too dry or wet.
SEASON Effective in spring. **BB**

Primula 'Francisca'

This has wonderful crinkled green flowers with pale yellow eyes. Like most green flowers, the flower heads look good for many months, probably because they photosynthesise and behave like leaves. The horticultural world has had green primroses before, but those I've bought have been around too long: many have been propagated with their concomitant viruses, weakening them. This is different and has enormous vigour. It was found in about 1995 by Francisca Darts on a traffic island in Canada, whence she bravely rescued it from sure oblivion.

HEIGHT/SPREAD 18 x 25cm.
ORIGINS Hybrid discovered in Canada.
CONDITIONS Fronts of borders. Like most primroses, it prefers neutral or acid soil.
SEASON Flowers from March to July. **BB**

Ribes x gordonianum

The choice of beautiful plants to grow is too great to bother with the demanding ones. This is an *easy* shrub. It is a hybrid between *Ribes sanguineum* and *R. odoratum*, made by Donald Beaton in 1837. He named it after his employer, William Gordon. It inherits scent from its mother, *R. odoratum*, and has flowers with apricot-yellow insides and soft red outsides – broadly midway between the flower colours of its parents. Its growth habit is neatish – certainly neater than the rather rangy *R. odoratum*. The flowering period is only about five weeks but the beauty of the flowers makes up for this.

HEIGHT/SPREAD 1.5 x 2m.
ORIGINS The parents are from the Midwest and West of North America.
CONDITIONS Anywhere except full shade.
SEASON Spring. **BB**

Places to visit

John Hoyland recommends places to visit for a good display of plants in spring

April and May are the months to enjoy auriculas. Collecting and showing auriculas was popular with 19th-century factory workers, especially in the north of England. **The National Auricula and Primula Society** still organises shows around the country and these are the best places to see auriculas close up. www.auriculaandprimula.org.uk

Auricula Theatre at Calke Abbey

The National Trust has preserved what may be the country's oldest surviving auricula theatre, at **Calke Abbey** in Derbyshire, which is spectacular when filled with auriculas. Ticknall, Derby, Derbyshire DE73 7LE. Tel 01332 863822, www.nationaltrust.org.uk
Perhaps the most beautiful glasshouse in the world is the Davies Alpine

Omphalodes cappadocica 'Cherry Ingram'

Spring is the prime time for woodland plants: they flower before the canopy of leaves shuts out the sunlight. Magnificent now, they don't do much for the rest of the year, so plant them under deciduous shrubs or near later-flowering perennials. This has dull, evergreen foliage, but by the time it starts flowering the new leaves are also appearing, all fresh and apple-green, a cheerful match for the sprays of blue flowers. The buds open with a violet tinge, but at their peak the flowers are a strong true-blue.

HEIGHT/SPREAD 20cm x 40cm. AGM.

ORIGINS The garden cultivar of a Turkish species.

CONDITIONS Will grow in light shade in all but very boggy soils.

SEASON March to April. **JH**

Muscari macrocarpum 'Golden Fragrance'

I like the ease with which muscari grow, so I make no excuses for including two kinds. This one is so good that Dutch nurseryman Wim de Goede has paid to have it patented, so I am not allowed to propagate it for resale – and it is good. The strong perfume makes me stop and breathe deeply. According to my wife, most grape hyacinths smell of cheap soap. This one has a sophisticated, sweet, rich musky, fruity perfume. The flower buds, held in a large spike, are dusky purple and change to yellow as they open. Even the grey-green foliage, arising with the flowers, doesn't let it down.

HEIGHT/SPREAD 15 x 10cm.

ORIGINS The Aegean and Western Turkey.

CONDITIONS Hot, dry, sunny places.

SEASON Flowers March to May. **BB**

Helleborus 'Anna's Red'

These plants possess the desirable quality of staring you right in the eye rather than shrinking away in the undergrowth. Dark stems rise up from lightly marbled leaves carrying gently overlapping, wide-brimmed sepals saturated in rich carmine red. These surround a centre of rolled lime green nectaries punctuated by chalky green stamens. Makes your mouth water and if they are half as special as Anna Pavord herself then you're on to a winner. Planted at Great Dixter among the silver leaves of *Pulmonarias*, I hope it has the background it needs.

HEIGHT/SPREAD 35cm x 30cm.

ORIGINS Bred by Rodney Davey of RD Plants, Devon, and named after Anna Pavord.

CONDITIONS Rich soil in semi shade.

SEASON February to March. **FG**

House at **The Royal Botanic Gardens, Kew**. The display of alpines is constantly changing and at this time of year there are always pots of interesting dwarf bulbs. Kew, Richmond, Surrey TW9 3AB. Open most days. Tel 020 8332 5655, www.kew.org

The Alpine house at the **Royal Botanic Gardens, Edinburgh** is more traditional but just as fascinating. Around the house there are sinks and troughs planted with alpines that can withstand life outdoors. 20A Inverleith Row, Edinburgh EH3 5LR. Open Open most days. Tel 0131 248 2909, www.rbge.org.uk

Many parks have exuberant plantings of tulips. Some of the most tasteful are by gardeners of the Royal Parks in **Regent's Park**, London. www.royalparks.org.uk

Tulips at Pashley Manor

Bloms Bulbs do mass tulip show plantings at Constable Burton, Yorkshire, Chenies Manor, Hertfordshire and most spectacularly, at **Pashley Manor,** Ticehurst, near Wadhurst, East Sussex TN5 7HE. Seasonal opening. Tel 01580 200888, www. pashleymanorgardens.com or www.blomsbulbs.com/ shows

Tulipa turkestanica

A profuse, free-flowering, multi-headed tulip, standing 20cm tall with delicately fragrant, creamy white starry flowers, carried on several lazily arranged stems. The flowers are made up of six pointed petals – each of which is marked with a broad yellow blotch at its base. These collectively create a vivid sunny centre as the blooms splay open on a warm day. The outsides of the flowers and the tips of the thin elegant stems are washed in shades of grey-green. Swollen, club shaped, streaked seedheads follow. The dried bulbs are beautiful too, resembling small shallots wrapped in brick red sheaths.

HEIGHT/SPREAD **20cm x 20cm.** AGM.

ORIGINS **Central Asia: Tien Shan Mountains through to north- west China, growing in stony slopes and rocky ledges.**

CONDITIONS **Sunny, with well-drained soil.**

SEASON **February to March or March to April. FG**

Bergenia 'Bressingham White'

A robust growth habit and tolerance of relatively poor soil have pushed bergenias towards the category of 'amenity landscape material'. This is unfortunate, when so much marks them out for recognition. Norfolk nursery Blooms of Bressingham clearly agreed, and bred a range of bergenias with good flower and foliage features. This one has creamy white flowers, each clasped in a waxy pink calyx. The evergreen foliage stays neater than most, though trimming old leaves in February makes way for a clean break in spring.

HEIGHT/SPREAD 30cm x 30cm. AGM.
ORIGINS Central and eastern Asia.
CONDITIONS Most garden loams; benefits from an application of leaf mulch in spring to encourage new foliage.
SEASON Flowers February to March. **CM**

Cyclamen coum

This hails from the southern Balkans to the Middle East. Its delicate looks belie its ruggedness. The luminosity of its propeller-like flowers – in white, pink or carmine, on 10cm stems – cheers the late winter months. The rounded leaves are remarkably diverse: bold or subtly patterned, sometimes plain deep green or leaden silver grey, as in the Pewter Group. It should be surface-planted in generous drifts and demands free drainage, a little shade and a vow not to spear the summer dormant tubers with your misguided fork.

HEIGHT/SPREAD 10cm x 8cm. AGM.
ORIGINS From Bulgaria to Turkey, Iran and as far south as Lebanon.
CONDITIONS Likes moderately fertile, humus-rich, well-drained soil.
SEASON Flowers in late winter and early spring. **GG**

"A plant you smell before you see it. Antiseptic notes of perfume carry on the air and rounding a corner in the garden I am confronted by a well-clothed, rounded bush laden with unfolding blossoms"

Mahonia aquifolium 'Smaragd'

Pulmonaria 'Cotton Cool'

Many of the early herbaceous plants reward us with decorative foliage at this time, none more so than the pulmonarias. I have been impressed by the vigour and reliability of this selection, where the characteristic silvered marking is almost entire on the leaves. The shimmering hummocks expand rapidly given half-favourable conditions and are studded with plentiful flowers. The display of young foliage can be repeated if they are sheared off after flowering to encourage fresh growth.

HEIGHT/SPREAD 20cm x 30cm.
ORIGINS Bred by Diana Grenfell at Apple Court Nursery.
CONDITIONS Prefers soil humus-rich and moisture-retentive, but copes with worse.
SEASON Flowers March to April, but repeats foliage if cut back. **CM**

Mahonia aquifolium 'Smaragd'

A plant you smell before you see it. Antiseptic notes of *Mahonia* perfume carry on the air and rounding a corner in the garden I am confronted by a well-clothed, rounded bush laden with unfolding blossoms. When other mahonias perished in the freezing winter of 2010, this stood unflinching through -18°C to emerge without blemish. I prefer blossoms in semi-mature state when they display a tonal range from primrose yellow to glorious gold across buds and exploded blooms on each floret. A magnet for early bees.

HEIGHT/SPREAD 1.3m x 1.3m.
ORIGINS North America.
CONDITIONS Happy in most soils, including clay.
SEASON March to April. **CM**

Euphorbia x martini Tiny Tim (='Waleutiny')

The one thing I don't like about this plant is the name, which suggests a diminutive form and rather sickly constitution. Far from it – this shade-tolerant evergreen is reliably robust and adds valuable structure to winter plantings. Juvenile spring foliage emerges with attractive reddish tones, balancing the characteristic lime-green inflorescence which make up the euphorbia flowers. Arising as a cross between sun-loving *Euphorbia characias* and shade-tolerant *E. amygdaloides*, the plant is adaptable to a wide range of conditions, and the more compact habit obviates any need for staking – or crutches.

HEIGHT/SPREAD 60cm x 90cm.
ORIGINS A hybrid of two European species.
CONDITIONS Humus-rich soil, sun or shade.
SEASON Flowers March to May. **CM**

Places to visit

Chris Marchant shares some of her favourite gardens and other places to see plants at their best

The Daffodil Meadow at **Exbury Gardens** in Hampshire is a glorious, cheering sight on a sunny day, and if you are lucky you'll probably catch some of the early rhododendrons and camellias, too. In all the gardens comprise 200 acres, established by Lionel de Rothschild between the two world wars. Finish your visit with a trip to the plant centre

Exbury Gardens

to secure some mementoes. Exbury Gardens, Exbury, Southampton SO45 1AZ. Seasonal opening. Tel 023 8089 9422, www.exbury.co.uk
Hodsock Priory has an enchanting woodland garden brimming with snowdrops, cyclamen and aconites. Coloured stems of dogwood, birch and willow are reflected around the lake, and hellebore

Veronica umbrosa 'Georgia Blue'

When other plants are showing tips above soil, this *Veronica* has galloped ahead and spread a bronzy skirt of foliage across the ground. I value this one not as a border plant but as a foil for more structured planting and an early detail for rockery or scree plantings. Where I have them in a planter on the north side of the house, they encircle the giant buds of *Hosta* 'Sum and Substance'. Their trailing stems quickly extend to form a floral curtain that endures for three weeks, by which time the hosta has unfurled to take centre stage.

HEIGHT/SPREAD 15cm x 30cm.

ORIGINS Caucasus, Turkey and Ukraine; Roy Lancaster introduced this cultivar.

CONDITIONS Well-drained soil in sun or light shade.

SEASON March to April. **CM**

Sempervivum arachnoideum

On a fine March morning it's encouraging to take coffee in the garden. It's too early for big floral displays, but a bowl of these on the table reminds us of nature's resilience. These perfectly formed rosettes form a spiky tapestry covered with a spider's web of fine hairs. Plentiful off-shoots can be planted in a container for next season. In some places sempervivums are grown on roofs. In ancient times, this was thought to guard against sorcery and to ensure the prosperity of the occupants.

HEIGHT/SPREAD 12cm x 10cm. AGM.

ORIGINS Mountainous parts of central and southern Europe and Mediterranean islands.

CONDITIONS Free-draining, sandy soil.

SEASON Evergreen foliage; flowers in April. **CM**

Helleborus x hybridus 'Picotee'

Working at Washfield Nursery with Elizabeth Strangman introduced me to the patience needed to breed plants at the highest level. I was on the scene during this hellebore's early development, to witness years of patient crossing, backcrossing and rigorous selection – taking three years from pollination to flowering. With its cupped flowers, purple-stained sepals and ruff of purple nectaries, the 'Picotee' strain is a favourite and stands as a testament to one of the country's finest plant breeders.

HEIGHT/SPREAD 45cm x 45cm.

ORIGINS Hybrid of *H. orientalis*, a species from Greece and Turkey.

CONDITIONS Tolerates all but dry or poorly-drained soils.

SEASON Flowers mid-winter to mid-spring. **GG**

Hodsock Priory

banks and well-stocked ferneries complete the circuit. Blyth, Nottinghamshire S81 0TY. Hodsock Priory holds open days for snowdrops (February) and bluebells (May). Tel 01909 591 204, www.hodsockpriory.com

For those who prefer to garden on a smaller scale, **Waterperry Gardens** stages a Saxifrage Weekend each March. Waterperry has a long

tradition of growing Alpine saxifrages dating back to the 1930s. The garden holds National Collections of Kabschia saxifrage (at their best in March) and Silver saxifrages (best in May-June). The excellent tearoom is renowned for its home baking. Wheatley, Oxfordshire OX33 1JZ. Open most days. Tel 01844 339254, www. waterperrygardens.co.uk

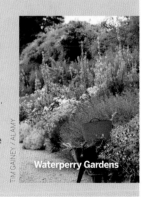

Waterperry Gardens

Lathyrus vernus

This is an underrated spring perennial, perhaps because of its alliance with the common vetch. From neat basal clumps emerge wiry stems bearing 6-10 hooded flowers, characteristic in shape of the pea family, but without tendrils, so not intent on scrambling through neighbouring plants. Flattish emerald pods follow; these ripen to a glorious red before snapping open and jettisoning seeds in all directions. Not content to stay meekly where originally placed, this plant contributes uncertainty to woodland layouts – just as nature intended.

HEIGHT/SPREAD 35cm x 30cm. AGM.
ORIGINS Woods, scrub and rocky ledges of most of Europe.
CONDITIONS Tolerates most loam soils; mulch with organic matter in spring.
SEASON Late March to April. **CM**

Primula veris

Where did all the cowslips go? As a child I remember them being as common as bluebells: bright and chipper, lining the lane to school. In a few parts of Britain country lanes are still bordered with primroses and cowslips, but those of us in the rest of country have to plant our own. Plant lots, not only because they look better in drifts, but because that way you can smell their sweet perfume without getting down on all fours. Collect the ripe seed and sow it immediately or simply sprinkle it around.

HEIGHT/SPREAD 25cm x 25cm. AGM.
ORIGINS Throughout temperate Europe and parts of Asia.
CONDITIONS Prefers a light soil but will grow in most conditions.
SEASON April. **JH**

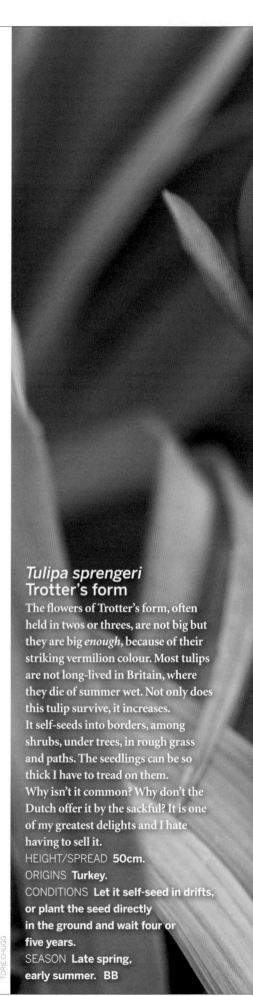

Tulipa sprengeri
Trotter's form

The flowers of Trotter's form, often held in twos or threes, are not big but they are big *enough*, because of their striking vermilion colour. Most tulips are not long-lived in Britain, where they die of summer wet. Not only does this tulip survive, it increases. It self-seeds into borders, among shrubs, under trees, in rough grass and paths. The seedlings can be so thick I have to tread on them. Why isn't it common? Why don't the Dutch offer it by the sackful? It is one of my greatest delights and I hate having to sell it.

HEIGHT/SPREAD **50cm.**
ORIGINS **Turkey.**
CONDITIONS **Let it self-seed in drifts, or plant the seed directly in the ground and wait four or five years.**
SEASON **Late spring, early summer. BB**

"Tulip-shaped buds of rich reddish purple open into fat goblet-shaped flowers revealing a white and pale-pink inside, highlighted by a protruding prehistoric cone of brown carpels and pink stamens"

Magnolia 'Galaxy'

Magnolia 'Galaxy'

Tulip-shaped buds of rich reddish purple open into fat goblet-shaped flowers revealing a white and pale-pink inside, highlighted by a protruding prehistoric cone of brown carpels and pink stamens. The flowers arrive before the leaves on this stark, grey-barked, single-stemmed, low hung tree. The shape becomes wider and more conical as its arching branches droop with age. The display is a sumptuous spectacle. The large oval leaves turn muddied yellow in autumn.

HEIGHT/SPREAD 8-10m x 4-8m. AGM.
ORIGINS Bred in United States National Arboretum, Washington DC, in 1963.
CONDITIONS Sun or light shade in a sheltered position in moist and humus-rich soil. Avoid chalk.
SEASON March into April. **FG**

SHARON PEARSON

Cornus mas

Cultivated for centuries in Europe and Asia, the Cornelian cherry dogwood has provided man with wood for tooling, bark for dyeing, acidic red fruits for preserving and uses in medicine. A large, open shrub, its yellow, four-petalled flowers, clustered on bare twiggy branches, cannot compete with exotic, larger spring blooms, and require careful placing and the help of other humble plants – a carpet of primroses, *Anemone apennina* and spotted lungworts, perhaps. Purple leaves in autumn and different berry/leaf forms are bonuses.

HEIGHT/SPREAD 5m x 5m.
ORIGINS Europe and western Asia.
CONDITIONS Deep, moderately fertile, well-drained soil.
SEASON Yellow flowers in spring, edible red fruits in summer and purple autumn foliage. **GG**

SHARON PEARSON

Lamium orvala

It is the scale of this plant that makes me smile. We are all familiar with the humble dead nettle of English ditches and verges, but this giant form has aspirations of grandeur. To further its case, the flowers are not white but an elegant coppery pink with intricate burgundy veining. If it were an orchid, we would be marking its card high for presentation. The classic square-section lamium stem ensures no staking is required. Sought out by bees from miles around for its source of early pollen.

HEIGHT/SPREAD 60cm x 60cm.
ORIGINS Native to scrubs and maquis in central southern Europe.
CONDITIONS Most soils; partial to full shade.
SEASON April-May. **CM**

JASON INGRAM

Places to visit

Chris Marchant shares some of her favourite gardens and other places to see plants at their best

A trip to Nottingham at this time should include a visit to the medieval manor house of **Holme Pierrepont Hall**, where you can venture to outlying fields and take in the splendour of *Tulipa sylvestris* naturalised in great multitudes. Holme Pierrepoint, Nottinghamshire NG12 2LD. The garden opens on various days from February to April.

Holme Pierrepont Hall

DETAIL NOTTINGHAM / ALAMY

Tel 0115 933 2371, www.holmepierreponthall.com

The jewel-like precision of auricula primulas has led to their being collected and displayed in formal 'theatre' stagings for hundreds of years. Gardeners in the north of England might care to visit the walled gardens in **Temple Newsam Estate** east of Leeds. Here, amid 1,500 acres of landscaped parkland, there

Melica altissima 'Alba'

Although relatively simple and seemingly unglamorous in its own right, this plant has the capacity to bring alive a range of informal border compositions. There are tactile and kinetic elements to its charm. Flowers like grains of white rice are suspended on slender, wiry stems and tremble in the slightest breeze. I have threaded these plants through countless other woodland flowering plants to impart transparency and texture.

HEIGHT/SPREAD 60cm x 30cm.
ORIGINS Found in alkaline woodlands across Europe to Russia.
CONDITIONS Prefers well-drained alkaline to neutral soil in shady aspect. Drought tolerant but resents excessive winter wet.
SEASON April to June. **CM**

Erysimum cheiri 'Blood Red'

This deliciously scented wallflower needs little qualification to justify inclusion. Strictly speaking a short-lived sub shrub, in the UK gardeners tend to grow them as hardy biennials, bedding out in late autumn in readiness for the following spring. The fragrance is strongest after an April shower, when still air is gently warmed by sun. Velvet-textured, dark red flowers make an exciting contrast with tulips. We use 'Blood Red' in formal planters on the terrace where they scramble through orange *Tulipa* 'Irene' or the redder *T.* 'Jan Reus'.

HEIGHT/SPREAD 50cm x 30cm.
ORIGINS The species grows across temperate zones of Europe.
CONDITIONS Copes with a wide range of soils but prefers well-drained loam.
SEASON Flowers March-April. **CM**

Salix hastata 'Wehrhahnii'

Some plants bring a welcome tactile appeal to the garden border, and this is one. A slow-growing willow with even, spreading habit, that achieves only modest proportions even when fully grown and is therefore suitable for gardens great and small. In spring, stout, dark twigs are generously covered with silken, silvery male buds. Each one expands into an explosion of golden catkins, supported by fresh green foliage. At its flowering peak it is hard to resist a touch as you pass.

HEIGHT/SPREAD 1m x 1m. AGM.
ORIGINS Northern Europe.
CONDITIONS Moisture-retentive soil in sun or light shade.
SEASON Spectacular catkins in April, leaf cover thereafter. **CM**

are six National Collections, including one of alpine primula auriculas. The Walled Garden, Temple Newsam Estate, Leeds LS15 0AD. Free entry to the estate most days. Tel 0113 336 7560, email mark.darwell@leeds.gov.uk (Mark is the National Collections co-ordinator, Leeds City Council.)

On selected days in late spring and early summer, **The**

Old Rectory, Farnborough, once the home to the late Poet Laureate John Betjeman is now owned by Caroline and Michael Todhunter. In a series of garden rooms, the imaginative and accomplished planting combinations grow in formal and informal areas, with woodland walks especially good at this time – the multitude of *Allium ursinum*

Old Rectory, Farnborough

cascading in a white froth is a sight to behold. Borders have many rare and interesting plants. The four-acre garden also has a collection of old roses and clematis, and wild flowers line the front lawn by the ha-ha. Farnborough, Wantage, Oxon, Berks OX12 8NX. Open under the National Gardens Scheme. www.ngs.org.uk

Summer

In May the garden is filled with lush green growth and by July the flower beds have finally filled out and are ablaze with colour. Celebrate all the moods of summer with our selection of fabulous plants for a fresh new look in your garden

Veronicastrum virginicum 'Pointed Finger'

Veronicastrums are impeccably behaved perennials with tapered flower spikes in lavender blue, mauve, pink or white. *V. virginicum* 'Pointed Finger' is shown here with *Sanguisorba officinalis* 'Pink Tanna'.

HEIGHT/SPREAD **1.5m x 45cm.**

ORIGINS **'Pointed Finger' is a cultivated form of a North American species.**

CONDITIONS **All soils, including clay.**

SEASON **Flowers June to early autumn; seedheads look striking in winter. GG**

Lupinus 'Masterpiece'

I am not normally a lupin lover, being rather scathing of their vulnerability to lupin aphid and of their 'all or nothing' habit, leaving ugly gaps in the border after flowering. But this is not a normal lupin. 'Masterpiece' is aptly named. Giant aubergine-purple flower spikes open in ascending sequence, offering a vision of lime green and purple for several days until the blooms are fully opened. It's pictured in our garden with white *Allium* 'Mount Everest' and a catmint that arose as a chance seedling, which we have named *Nepeta* 'Tapdance'.

HEIGHT/SPREAD **1m x 45cm.**

ORIGINS **Bred by Sarah Conibear of Westcountry Nurseries in Devon and distributed under licence.**

CONDITIONS **Well-drained, neutral to acid soil. Dislikes spring drought while in growth and needs protection from winter wet.**

SEASON **Flowers from May to June. CM**

JASON INGRAM

Trollius x *cultorum* 'Alabaster'

In spring a chorus of yellows brightens our pond: *Caltha*, *Iris pseudacorus* and *Trollius*. Which is why this paler, cream-flowering *Trollius* earns a mention. The perfect globular buds are fat and promising. Each snug petal is delicately outlined with a trace of pink, unfolding to reveal double flowers with a glorious ivory sheen. These grow easily among natives such as shuttlecock fern (*Matteuccia struthiopteris*) and meadowsweet (*Filipendula vulgaris*).
HEIGHT/SPREAD 65cm x 30cm.
ORIGINS Trollius come from damp meadows of Europe, N Asia and N America. 'Alabaster' was bred by the Arends Nursery, Germany.
CONDITIONS Moisture-retentive, loamy soil.
SEASON May to June. **CM**

JASON INGRAM

JASON INGRAM

Silene dioica 'Firefly'

Introduced by Norfolk nursery Blooms of Bressingham, this red campion cultivar is sterile, so has none of the spreading tendencies of many *Silene* species. When striving towards a balanced composition in the garden border, I prefer the brightest of flowers to be relatively small. This is unashamedly bright pink, and all the more glorious for it. I love the intensity of the tight, double flowers, branched and airy on upright stems and use it sparingly to accent the deeper, more moody violets of salvias and *Geranium phaeum*.
HEIGHT/SPREAD 80cm x 25cm.
ORIGINS *Silene dioica* is native to northern temperate regions of Europe.
CONDITIONS A wide range of free-draining soils, preferably neutral to alkaline.
SEASON May to June. **CM**

"Giant aubergine-purple flower spikes open in ascending sequence, offering a vision of lime green and purple for several days until the blooms are fully opened"

Lupinus 'Masterpiece'

Salvia pratensis 'Lapis Lazuli'

Its name is an anomaly, since its flowers are not the electric blue of lazurite. But it is one of the earliest of salvias to send up its large, hooded flowers of lipstick-pink. If you seek robust and dry-tolerant colour in a sunny, lean soil, this ticks all the boxes. Moreover, you can have not one, but two flowering seasons each year, if you cut back spent flower stems in late May. At the nursery we keep these plants in a windy spot where watering is light. Undeterred, they stand strong, tall and upright.

HEIGHT/SPREAD 65cm x 40cm.
ORIGINS *Salvia pratensis* is widely distributed across Europe to Russia.
CONDITIONS Tolerant of broad range of well-drained loamy soils in a sunny aspect.
SEASON May to June and again in August to September. **CM**

Camassia leichtlinii 'Semiplena'

A modest outlay on bulbs can make an impressive display in grassland or orchards. This semi-double form has much to recommend it, including long-lasting flowers. Opening two weeks later than straight *C. leitchlinii*, its flowers last around twice as long. The flowers are of a delectable greenish ivory hue, fading up the long stem to a warm bronzy brown. The overall effect is attractive in bud, flower and decline. Flowers are sterile, so multiplication of clumps is by expansion and division, which helps to keep the flowering display on form.

HEIGHT/SPREAD Up to 1m x 35cm.
ORIGINS Western North America.
CONDITIONS Tolerant of dappled shade and heavy soils; needs moist soil in spring.
SEASON Late May to June. **CM**

Papaver orientale Goliath Group 'Beauty of Livermere'

There may be exuberant showgirl qualities about the flowers of the Oriental poppies, but many of them flower only briefly, or collapse on over-laden stems. With this form, stems are straight, upright and true, rising a good 50cm above the mound of foliage. Giant single blooms unfold to deepest blood red. We nestle them among the beetroot-coloured foliage of annual *Atriplex hortensis* var. *rubra*, which frames the blooms before obligingly rising up to conceal them after flowering.

HEIGHT/SPREAD Up to 110cm x 80cm.
ORIGINS The species is from eastern Turkey, northern Iran and the Caucasus Mountains.
CONDITIONS Well-drained, fertile loam.
SEASON Flowers May to June. **CM**

Places to visit

Chris Marchant shares some of her favourite gardens and other places to see plants at their best.

Ascott House is a National Trust property offering 30 acres of Victorian planting detail originally laid out by nurseryman Sir Harry Veitch and subsequently expanded along more contemporary lines. In the spring visitors are indulged with colourful carpets of bulbs. There is also a significant collection of fine trees set in parkland. Leighton Buzzard, Bedfordshire

A carpet of bulbs at Ascott, Leighton Buzzard.

LU7 0PR. Seasonal opening. Tel 01296 688242, www.nationaltrust.co.uk

The classic William Kent garden at **Rousham House** in Oxfordshire is a favourite at almost any point in the year. At this time, the wonderful apple orchard comes into its own. Step through the door into a cloud of scented blossom. The 27-acre gardens have all the majesty of a fine

Geranium phaeum 'Lily Lovell'

This carries all the robust and trouble-free qualities of the *Geranium phaeum* species, but is distinct in the curious colour of the flowers, which open violet and fade to almost navy blue. I find this shade more uplifting than the sombre maroon of the native lady in mourning and a marvellous companion to all the lime greens and creams of spring. We use this threaded through Solomon's seal (*Polygonatum* x *hybridum*) and sweet cicely (*Myrrhis odorata*) on the wilder fringes.

HEIGHT/SPREAD 75cm x 30cm.
ORIGINS Mountainous regions of southern and central Europe; naturalised in UK. Cultivar introduced by geranium expert Trevor Bath.
CONDITIONS Most well-drained garden soils, from mildly acidic to alkaline.
SEASON May to June. **CM**

Bupleurum longifolium 'Bronze Beauty'

I first came upon this plant in the gardens of John Coke at Bury Court, in an area not generally on view. There, working in partnership with landscape architect Christopher Bradley-Hole, John has created an exciting tension between crisp, precise architecture and his own exuberant planting, which swells to great volume within the grid-like arrangement of formal beds. The colour palette is largely green, but scattered through are occasional jewels of flower shape and colour, all the better for being used sparingly.

HEIGHT/SPREAD 70cm x 30cm.
ORIGINS From central Europe into Siberia.
CONDITIONS Most well-drained soil in sun or light shade.
SEASON May to July. **CM**

Smyrnium perfoliatum

This subject has all the appeal of an uninvited but very entertaining guest at a party. Our frustrated efforts to grow it in pots under controlled conditions mean that we have not yet managed to offer it for sale from the nursery. But, given the right shady, humus-rich woodland conditions in the garden, freely scattered seeds from this plant offer reasonable germination. In return, they will reward handsomely with a chorus of glorious limey flower heads in the spring.

HEIGHT/SPREAD Up to 70cm x 30cm.
ORIGINS Europe and Caucasus.
CONDITIONS Humus-rich, moisture-retentive soil in dappled shade.
SEASON Flowers May to June. **CM**

landscaped space, with niches of intimacy. Near Steeple Aston, Bicester OX25 4QX. Garden open most days. Tel 01869 347110, www. rousham.org

The Manor in Hemingford Grey is one of the oldest inhabited houses in the country. Lucy Boston, author of the Green Knowe children's stories, moved here in 1939 and created a 4.5-acre garden with the help of horticulturist Graham Stuart Thomas. A good collection of roses and the best of Sir Cedric Morris's irises were included in her schemes. Huntingdon, Cambridgeshire PE28 9BN. Garden is open most days of the year. Tel 01480 463134, www.greenknowe.co.uk

On a much smaller scale, **Weaver's Cottage** is home to Sylvia Norton and a National

The apple orchard at Rousham House.

Collection of sweet peas. But it is the owner's love of foxgloves that makes the garden a place of pilgrimage at this point in the season. 35 Streetly End, West Wickham, near Cambridge CB21 4RP. Seasonal opening by appointment and for the National Gardens Scheme. Tel 01223 892399, www.ngs.org.uk

Irises at The Manor, Hemingford Grey.

Thalictrum ichangense 'Purple Marble'

My inclination when presented with a new garden plant is to stand back and watch. Most fizzle into unavailability within five years, a few remain in circulation and some even become popular. This plant began to circulate in 2004 and it has a future. The foliage is amazing. Leaves are ternate – that is, with three leaflets, each of which is large, purple-stained and marbled with grey, mimicking a begonia. The flowers are fluffy and lilac and bloom continuously between April and October. A superb new garden plant.
HEIGHT/SPREAD 25-30cm x 25cm.
ORIGINS China.
CONDITIONS Ordinary shady or semi-shady places in open soil, not clay.
SEASON Particularly good in spring, but attrctive in summer as well. **BB**

Allium hollandicum 'Purple Sensation'

Selected for the size of the flower heads (like tennis balls) and their depth of colour. It bears large balls of flowers on violet-black pedicels from deep violet stems. They are supremely easy to grow and require no maintenance. I drop them in planting holes with other stuff (like phlox and geraniums) in autumn. The foliage appears in January and does its thing before its companion plant has woken up.
HEIGHT/SPREAD 1.2m. AGM.
ORIGINS Probably an old hybrid involving Central Asian species, done in Holland so long ago that no one remembers.
CONDITIONS Plant them in borders where they will not get winter shade.
SEASON May to July. **BB**

Akebia longeracemosa

Anything as exotic-looking as this ought not to survive outside in Britain, yet it prospers and flowers, climbing a plum tree in the middle of an exposed Midlands field. Although its commonly available cousin *Akebia quinata* would quickly smother its host, *A. longeracemosa* covers the tree sparsely, allowing both plants to coexist. The flowers smell of custard creams and dangle in grape-like heads topped by larger, red-black flowers. So I still have plums, but not yet the long, sausage-shaped, red-purple fruits of the *Akebia* – which are meant to be equally edible.
HEIGHT/SPREAD **3-5m x 3-5m.**
ORIGINS **Planthunters Bleddyn and Sue Wynne-Jones of Crûg Farm Plants collected my clone in northern Taiwan. It occurs in China as well.**
CONDITIONS **Sun and well-drained soil, with something to scramble up.**
SEASON **Early summer. BB**

"Clasped in grey calyxes, panicles of crisp-textured, rose-flushed white flowers festoon the cinnamon-toned flaking branches, creating an enthralling summer avalanche"

Deutzia pulchra

Deutzia pulchra

Deutzias tend to bring up the rear in the shrubbery owing to a reputation for being scentless, brief in flower and hangdog in appearance. Their cousins *Hydrangea* and *Philadelphus* shake off their faults more lightly. Redemption comes in the form of the handsome *D. pulchra* (meaning 'beautiful'). Its supposed tenderness is a myth: it is tough as nails but loves being ripened by the sun. Clasped in grey calyxes, panicles of crisp-textured, rose-flushed white flowers festoon the cinnamon-toned flaking branches, creating an enthralling summer avalanche.

HEIGHT/SPREAD 2.5m x 2m.
ORIGINS Taiwan, the Philippines.
CONDITIONS Any.
SEASON Flowers late spring to early summer; ornamental bark in winter. **GG**

RACHEL WARNE

Gladiolus papilio red form

Gladiolus papilio is a vigorous species whose bell-shaped lilac flowers are tinged with grey. In the wild the flowers are variable in colour, and I grow a beautiful red form that has butterfly-shaped markings on the inside of the flower. Another form, the pure red cultivar *G. papilio* 'Ruby', is supposed to have retained the hardiness of the species. During the cold winter of 2010 both the species and the red form survived in my garden. Unfortunately 'Ruby' died.

HEIGHT/SPREAD 50cm x 10cm.
ORIGINS Garden hybrid raised in New Zealand. The species grows in South Africa.
CONDITIONS Rich, well-drained soil in sun.
SEASON July. **JH**

Dierama pulcherrimum 'Merlin'

Until reproduction in laboratories by tissue culture, it was nearly impossible to buy dieramas and get the colour you wanted. Propagation by seed from richly coloured plants usually produced more washed-out colours, and reproduction by division caused plants to sulk. The colour everybody wanted was blackberry, in the cultivar 'Blackbird'. Now anyone can have the deep black-red of 'Merlin'. Good thing too. The flowers drip from slender stems that constantly move in the breeze.

HEIGHT/SPREAD 1m high and extending to 1m wide after ten years or so.
ORIGINS South Africa.
CONDITIONS Well-drained soil and not dry.
SEASON Flowers in midsummer. **BB**

SHARON PEARSON

TORIE CHUGG

Places to visit

John Hoyland recommends places to visit for a good display of plants in summer

Overlooking Lake Windermere and with the high peaks of the Lake District in the background, **Holehird Gardens** must have one of the most beautiful settings in Britain. The 17-acre hillside garden is packed with plants and is always beautifully maintained. Holehird is the home of the Lakeland Horticultural Society and

Holehird Gardens

ASHLEY COOPER / ALAMY

is gardened entirely by volunteers. Patterdale Road, Windermere, Cumbria LA23 1NP. Open most days. Tel 015394 46008, www. holehirdgardens.org.uk

Half-an-hour drive south of Holehird are the gardens of **Levens Hall**. Dating back to the late 17th century, the garden has some of the country's finest topiary. The box-edged beds are planted

Dianthus deltoides 'Leuchtfunk'

Representing blood, fire and power, red is the most emotive colour, exciting us and terrifying us. Through millennia its use in costume, both political and social, has served to exalt status: in painting it has heightened drama. And so it is in the garden, where a red flower never goes unnoticed. The diminished scale of this *Dianthus* belies the high drama of its intensely coloured flowers: Hitchcockian drops of blood on a carpet of green add to that effect, the scariest red of all.

HEIGHT/SPREAD 20cm x 30cm.
ORIGINS *D. deltoides* grows wild in Europe; this cultivar arose in a German nursery.
CONDITIONS Well drained; loamy or sandy.
SEASON Evergreen foliage, with flowers that last all summer. **GG**

Eryngium x zabelii

Blue flowers always seem to be enticing to gardeners, especially the sparkling metallic blue of the sea hollies. The intensity of the blue colouring varies between species and can change with growing conditions. In general, the bluest flowers are on plants grown in poor soils and in hot conditions. I find, though, that *E.* x *zabelii* is consistently blue, even crowded in the border and growing in rich soil. The name is given to hybrids of *E. bourgatii* and *E. alpinum*. The plants available for sale are variable but are characterised by strong, dark blue stems and large blue bracts.

HEIGHT/SPREAD 75cm x 25cm.
ORIGINS Garden hybrid.
CONDITIONS Well-drained soil in full sun.
SEASON July and August. **JH**

Rosa 'Geranium' (moyesii hybrid)

Introduced by Ernest 'Chinese' Wilson from northwest China in 1903 and named after his missionary friend Rev J Moyes, today this variable, vigorous species rose is best known in its red forms, in particular 'Geranium', raised at Wisley in 1938. A crown of golden stamens lies at the heart of each single, rich red, scentless flower. These deck the delicately leaved thicket of viciously thorned stems in a lavish display. The flowers' metamorphosis into bright orange-red hips brings autumn to a glowing close.

HEIGHT/SPREAD 2.4m x 1.5m. AGM.
ORIGINS Kanding, China.
CONDITIONS Tolerates poorer soils than many roses. Will also thrive in partial shade.
SEASON Flowers in summer and bears orange-red hips in autumn. **GG**

en-masse with single plants to create large blocks of colour in patterns. Levens Hall, Kendal, Cumbria LA8 0PD. Seasonal opening. Tel 015395 60321, www.levenshall.co.uk

Michael Wickenden's collection of plants at **Cally Gardens** is always exciting. The plants he sells are beautifully displayed in the gardens. Gatehouse of Fleet,

Castle Douglas DG7 2DJ. Seasonal opening. Tel 01557 815029, www.callygardens.co.uk

A short distance away is **Ellenbank**, the garden and nursery of Elizabeth and Alasdair MacGregor. Elizabeth is known for her collection of violas but Ellenbank is bursting with many more interesting plants. Tongland Road,

Ellenbank garden and nursery

Kirkcudbright DG6 4UU. Seasonal opening. Tel 01557 330620, www.elizabethmacgregor nursery.co.uk

From there you could go to **Buckland Plants** for rare woodlanders. The School, Whinnieliggate, Kirkcudbright DG6 4XP. Seasonal opening. Tel 01557 331323, www. bucklandplants.co.uk

Potentilla 'Volcan'

I love the use of red in summer plantings, and this deep blood red has to be one of my favourite ways of giving a dash of excitement to a sedate and sober composition. With their velvety texture and rich deep hue, the flowers of *Potentilla* 'Volcan' will scramble through branches of adjacent plants in their quest for light. It is particularly good associated with *Salvia verticillata* 'Purple Rain' and *Nepeta racemosa* 'Blue Wonder' to give a rich Persian carpet combination. The display lasts longer than many of the other herbaceous potentilla and this plant requires little attention to thrive.

HEIGHT/SPREAD **45cm x 35cm.**

ORIGINS **A hybrid of Potentilla atrosanguinea from high altitude scrub between Sikkim and Afghanistan.**

CONDITIONS **Most free-draining garden loams in a sunny position.**

SEASON **Flowers June to July. CM**

Euphorbia oblongata

This short-lived perennial has a giant propensity to self-seed – you can hear the 'ping' of exploding capsules on a warm day. This generally ensures continuity of the clump, though perhaps not in exactly the same place. There is a refreshing brightness in the openly expansive flower heads. Their acid green bracts tone effectively with almost any neighbouring plant and neatly infiltrate spaces in a young border. Sarah Raven has highlighted its value for cutting, rating it her number one foliage plant and mixing stems with sweet peas, roses or dahlias. For trouble-free impact and extended vase life, it earns high marks.

HEIGHT/SPREAD 60cm x 30cm.
ORIGINS Southern Europe.
CONDITIONS Well-drained garden loams.
SEASON June to September. **CM**

Nepeta subsessilis 'Washfield'

This was originally selected by plantswoman Elizabeth Strangman of Washfield Nursery. One could be forgiven for failing to recognise this as *Nepeta*, but its characteristic scent removes any doubt. A plant for grouping rather than edging, with dramatic flower heads of 15cm in length, it stands sturdy and upright. Even as the flowers fade and drop, the purple calyces remain entire and beautiful in their form, partnered by giant oval leaves, which acquire an attractive purple halo as the season progresses.

HEIGHT/SPREAD 70cm x 35cm.
ORIGINS *N. subsessilis* originates from damp, cooler, shady hillsides of S. Japan.
CONDITIONS Most fertile loam soils.
SEASON Flowers June to July, with foliage display into the autumn. **CM**

"This small, charming iris has earned itself the common epithet the plum tart iris since the flowers exude a curious sweet smell redolent of poached plums. The scent really conjures up a summer kitchen"

Iris graminea

Iris graminea

This plant has earned itself the common epithet the plum tart iris since the flowers exude a curious sweet smell redolent of poached plums. The scent really conjures up a summer kitchen. This is a small and charming iris with slender flowers whose colouring is a rich vignette of purples and mauve, enhanced by a characteristic metallic sheen. The falls are white, strongly veined with violet. *Iris graminea* has been awarded an RHS Award of Garden Merit.

HEIGHT/SPREAD 25cm x 15cm. AGM.
ORIGINS Native to grassy places and open woods of southern Europe.
CONDITIONS Moisture-retentive soil, preferring dappled shade in order to flower and to thrive.
SEASON Flowers May to June. **CM**

Libertia grandiflora

This plant is reliable and undemanding, while making a generous contribution to formal and informal assemblies. Even before the flowers appear, the slender sword-like foliage, arranged in fans, adds vertical definition to a scheme, provided you keep slugs and snails from decimating its precision. Arching flower stems bow down under the weight of startling white terminal flower clusters and give a lightened elegance to woodland scenes. Later, golden brown seed pods provide additional layers of interest.

HEIGHT/SPREAD 85cm x 50cm. AGM.
ORIGINS From stream banks and open woodlands in New Zealand.
CONDITIONS Prefers a humus-rich, fertile soil.
SEASON Flowers May and June. Seed heads extend the interest. **CM**

Campanula latifolia var. alba

This elegant campanula will take a range of conditions from open sun to dappled shade. Its tidy, clump-forming habit is easily managed among other plants, and upright stems rise invitingly above diminutive neighbours to take up flowering prominence once aquilegias and early geraniums have faded. Elongated flowers emerge from torpedo-like buds held in outward-facing arrangement up the stem. Out of shade, this plant makes a good companion to mid-season shrub roses.

HEIGHT/SPREAD 70cm x 30cm.
ORIGINS Native to European woodlands and meadows.
CONDITIONS Most fertile garden loams with some moisture retention, preferring neutral to alkaline conditions.
SEASON June. **CM**

Places to visit

Chris Marchant shares some of her favourite gardens and other places to see plants at their best

It can be good to challenge perceptions of what plants should be included in a border. The naturalistic approach of Strilli Oppenheimer, the owner of **Waltham Place**, assisted by the late Dutch plantsman Henk Gerritsen, has achieved a very different planting balance. The 40-acre organic garden includes potager, knot garden, herbaceous borders,

Waltham Place is famed for its long borders.

woods, lake and grass maze. An organic farm supplies produce for a café and shop. Waltham Place also runs training courses. White Waltham, Maidenhead SL6 3JH. Seasonal opening by appointment and under the National Gardens Scheme. Tel 01628 825517, www.walthamplace.com

Those familiar with the world of the late author Roald

Gillenia trifoliata

This adds movement to a planting scheme when caught by even the gentlest breeze. Don't be deceived by its diaphanous appearance; it has an iron constitution once established. It is good in association with shrub roses, offering a delightful airy contrast to the more weighty blooms. As plants fade, the foliage takes on autumnal tones of gold and burgundy and will contribute to a planting group for weeks.
HEIGHT/SPREAD 120cm x 50cm. AGM.
ORIGINS Native to open woods, clearings and road verges of eastern and south-eastern USA.
CONDITIONS Best in moist, humus-rich soil in full sun or light shade. Once established, it can withstand dryer seasons.
SEASON June to July. **CM**

Elaeagnus 'Quicksilver'

Where a silvered shrub is required to add an air of the Mediterranean to a cooler British garden, this hardy subject is sometimes used as a stand-in for *Olea*, earning it the common name of Russian olive. Its foliage is airy and well-spaced, and plants respond well to formative pruning. The small clusters of rather insignificant yellow flowers repay your patience when they open to give off their exquisite perfume. Positioning a bench near this shrub will encourage people to pause and to breathe deeply – which is no bad thing in any garden.
HEIGHT/SPREAD 80cm x 30cm. AGM.
ORIGINS Native to Western and Central Asia.
CONDITIONS Likes fertile, moisture-retentive soil.
SEASON June. **CM**

Delphinium requienii

Visitors to the Pangbourne garden of plantsman Bill Baker seldom emerged empty handed. When we remarked on some deeply fingered and shiny foliage emerging from the leaf mulch one spring, he introduced us to this biennial delphinium with the propensity to dissipate far and wide. We have never found it a pest, but allow plants to grow up where they are happiest. It needs no staking, and seems remarkably resistant to slug damage – unlike the more fragile perennial forms. We have come to rely on it to revive a fading *Paeonia* border in June.
HEIGHT/SPREAD 130cm to 150cm.
ORIGINS From the Isles d'Hyères (just south of France), Corsica and possibly Sardinia.
CONDITIONS Suitable for most loamy soils, and copes well even in dry.
SEASON June to July. **CM**

Dahl can visit the gardens of his former home, **Gipsy House**. An intriguing series of outdoor rooms is divided by hedges and walls. An avenue of pleached limes leads to his writing hut. Ornamental borders and a productive vegetable garden occupy the foreground, while magnificent floral meadows take your view out to the countryside. Gipsy House, Whitefield Lane, Great Missenden, Bucks HP16 0BP. Open on selected days under the National Gardens Scheme. www.ngs.org.uk

Nearby is a **Roald Dahl Museum** dedicated to the author, and aimed at 6 to 12-year olds. 81-83 High Street, Great Missenden, Bucks HP16 0AL. www.roalddahlmuseum.org.

Next door to Gipsy House garden is an excellent nursery

Gipsy House, the garden of the late Roald Dahl.

and display garden. **The Plant Specialist** has an extensive range of durable, new and unusual herbaceous perennials and grasses. There are seductive display areas and knowledgeable staff. Seasonal opening hours. 7 Whitfield Lane, Great Missenden, Bucks HP16 0BP. Tel 01494 866650, www.theplantspecialist.co.uk

Orlaya grandiflora

This bewitching annual brings diaphanous clouds of cow parsley into the garden without swamping everything. The flowers are a clear, bright white and resemble lace-cap hydrangeas. What look like enlarged petals around the edge of the flower act as landing pads for small insects. The popularity of this plant over the past few years has encouraged gardeners to return to sowing annuals. You usually find a few self-sown plants in the second year but the best policy is to sow afresh each year. You get larger, early-flowering plants from sowing in autumn and planting out after the frosts have gone.

HEIGHT/SPREAD 45cm x 10cm. AGM.
ORIGINS South, central and western Europe.
CONDITIONS Sun or part shade in all but very wet soils.
SEASON Flowers from May to July. **JH**

Cistus ladanifer 'Paladin'

During the early summer, the hills that sweep down to the Mediterranean at the eastern end of the Pyrenees are covered in *Cistus ladanifer*. They thrive on the poor, rocky soil and the baking heat. The straggly growth of the species is great on a craggy hillside but just looks untidy in the garden, so in Britain I grow a neat and compact cultivar, 'Paladin'. The fragile, tissue-paper flowers are ephemeral but plentiful. It has grown well in my garden for the last ten years but died in the wretched winter of 2010. I'll plant more in the optimistic hope that we won't see a winter like that for another decade.

HEIGHT/SPREAD 1.5m x 1.5m.
ORIGINS Western Mediterranean.
CONDITIONS Likes sun and poor, well-drained soil.
SEASON June to July. **JH**

"*This iris is so elegant it seems to be straight from a classical Chinese painting. The pencil-thin, branching stems are suffused with dark purple and the same colour seeps up from the base of the plant to stain the leaves*"

Iris x robusta 'Gerald Darby'

Iris x robusta 'Gerald Darby'

This iris is so elegant it seems to be straight from a classical Chinese painting. The pencil-thin, branching stems are suffused with dark purple and the same colour seeps up from the base of the plant to stain the leaves. The overall effect is very stylish. It will grow in shallow water and is often recommended as a plant for the edges of ponds. That is good advice if you have an estate with a large lake but it is far too vigorous for most domestic ponds. Keep it in the border, where it won't get out of hand.

HEIGHT/SPREAD **75cm x 50cm.** AGM.
ORIGINS **A hybrid of *I. versicolor* and *I. virginica*.**
CONDITIONS **Moist soil in sun.**
SEASON **June and July.** JH

Achillea Anthea (='Anblo')

Twenty years ago I used to grow *Achillea clypeolata*. A beautiful plant, it has delicate silvery foliage and grey buds. The whole effect was ruined, though, when the flowers appeared – a sharp and bitter acid yellow. Plant breeder Alan Bloom, always keen-eyed, spotted the plant's potential and used it to produce a hybrid with soft, faded-cream flowers. The silver foliage is now perfectly matched with the muted colours of the flowers. Bloom trademarked it *A. Anthea* after his daughter. The stems are thick and the plant compact, so it doesn't flop about like other achilleas.

HEIGHT/SPREAD 60cm x 30cm.
ORIGINS Bred by Blooms of Bressingham.
CONDITIONS Well-drained soil in full sun.
SEASON May to July. **JH**

Paeonia emodi

This is one of those plants that turns you into a show-off – at any rate mine has. When it is in flower even the postman gets dragged over to see it. The flowers are white, as delicate as tissue paper, and cover the plant's shiny green foliage. It is a beautiful sight. The new shoots start pushing through in February and are a dark olive and bronze colour. It is one of the few peonies that grows in shade (mine are under the canopy of a large bay tree). It sets seed but I also divide my plants every few years during August.

HEIGHT/SPREAD 1m x 1m.
ORIGINS North India, north Pakistan and Afghanistan.
CONDITIONS Shady woodland conditions.
SEASON Flowers in early May. **JH**

Buddleja alternifolia 'Argentea'

In the spring this shrub always looks untidy, with unruly stems growing every which way, but by June it is a cascade of flowers. The long, thin branches arch over almost to the ground and each is covered with lilac flowers that grow spirally along the stems. On mature plants the flower stems are several feet long. My plants are grown as standards but the weight of the flowers is such that the trunk has to be staked to support it. It is also impressive when trained to grow against a wall. This cultivar has silver-backed leaves that complement the colour of the flowers.

HEIGHT/SPREAD Up to 4m x 3m.
ORIGINS China.
CONDITIONS Sun or part-shade in well-drained soil.
SEASON June to July. **JH**

Places to visit

John Hoyland recommends places to visit for a good display of plants in summer.

Helmsley Walled Garden, midway between Pickering and Thirsk in North Yorkshire, is maintained by a charitable trust that provides horticultural therapy and training to disadvantaged young people. It is a beautifully maintained garden and home to hundreds of clematis cultivars. Cleveland Way, Helmsley, North Yorkshire YO62 5AH.

Helmsley Walled Garden

Seasonal opening. Tel 01439 771427, www.helmsleywalledgarden.org.uk
Right next to Helmsley is **Duncombe Park**, one of the best landscape gardens in the country, with 25 acres to explore. Apart from the later addition of formal parterres, the landscape remains much as it was when created in the 18th century. Helmsley, North Yorkshire YO62 5EB.

Eryngium giganteum

This is one of those plants that I never tire of, however much I see it. The spiky bracts and silvery cones on candelabra stems always look imposing. Don't be deterred by the young foliage: rounded and marbled, it seems improbable that it could eventually produce anything so eye-catching. It is monocarpic, dying after flowering, but produces masses of seed. Let it seed itself about but be ruthless in weeding out most of the seedlings. It looks far more effective when single plants are dotted randomly through a border rather than colonising swathes of it. Known to many gardeners as Miss Willmott's ghost.
HEIGHT/SPREAD 100cm x 30cm. AGM.
ORIGINS The Caucasus.
CONDITIONS Poor, well-drained soil, full sun.
SEASON June to August. **JH**

RACHEL WARNE

RACHEL WARNE

Geranium 'Sandrine'

Crossing the same plants can give different results. *Geranium psilostemon* crossed with *G.* 'procurrens' gave us *G.* 'Ann Folkard', a plant with long, wandering stems of yellow-green foliage and startling dark purple flowers that have an almost black centre. A few years later the same parents produced a more compact plant with similar flowers, *G.* 'Anne Thomson'. And now we have *G.* 'Sandrine', which is also less straggly but has flowers that are 5cm wide, twice the size of 'Ann Folkard'. The combination of purple flowers and golden foliage is not for the faint-hearted.
HEIGHT/SPREAD 40cm x 75cm. AGM
ORIGINS Bred in France by Thierry Delabroye of Pépinières Delabroye.
CONDITIONS Sun and well-drained soil.
SEASON June and July. **JH**

Salvia nemorosa 'Caradonna'

Be wary of claims about plants that will flower all summer long: few will, and long-flowering doesn't necessarily make a great garden plant. Bindweed will flower for weeks on end. *S. nemorosa* 'Caradonna', though, is an exceptional plant that flowers throughout the summer *and* is stunningly beautiful. The stems are dark purple and the flowers violet-blue. Together they create an intense colour that is particularly striking when you grow several plants together. Bees and hoverflies love the flowers. To keep it flowering even longer, cut down the flower spikes once they start to fade and new ones will spring up.
HEIGHT/SPREAD 50cm x 30cm. AGM.
ORIGINS Garden cultivar found in Germany.
CONDITIONS Sun and well-drained soil.
SEASON June to August. **JH**

RACHEL WARNE

Seasonal opening. Tel 01439 770213, www.duncombepark.com
The walled garden at nearby **Scampston Hall** is at its height later in the year but is impressive even now. The 4.5 acre garden, designed by Piet Oudolf, is divided into eight areas, with virtuoso planting schemes throughout. One of the areas has a mound that allows you to look down

on the garden to get a sense of the overall design. In contrast to the contemporary design and planting of the walled garden, Scampston Hall is set in a park laid out in the 1780s by Lancelot 'Capability' Brown. Malton, North Yorkshire YO17 8NG. Seasonal opening. Tel 01944 759111, www.scampston.co.uk
To buy plants while you

JOHN GLOVER / ALAMY

Scampston Hall

are in the area head down to **Stillingfleet Lodge Nursery**, south of York. The owner, Vanessa Cook, has unusual perennial plants that are reasonably priced. Allow plenty of time to visit the extensive gardens. Stewart Lane, Stillingfleet, York YO19 6HP. Seasonal opening. Tel 01904 728506, www.stillingfleetlodge nurseries.co.uk

Daucus carota

Looking through the spring meadow sward reveals the humble wild carrot, whose fern-like foliage is sustained by a probing, pallid, drought-resisting root. The progenitor of the plump root we crunch on, its herbal treatments are also legendary: flatulence among others. Caution prevails, for its lookalike, water hemlock, is deadly poisonous. An indispensable part of the meadow tapestry and an exceptional insect-magnet, *Daucus carota* flowers in June to August, often pink in bud opening to airy, shallow, white domes. The cocoon of dun-coloured seeds gives rise to the quaint vernacular name, bird's-nest plant.

HEIGHT/SPREAD **90cm x 30cm.**

ORIGINS **Europe.**

CONDITIONS **All soils.**

SEASON **Flowers between June and August. GG**

Agapanthus 'Marchants Cobalt Cracker'

Agapanthus species are South African in origin. Their promiscuous offspring have made them a nurseryman's favourite worldwide, resulting in a plethora of forms. Longevity and hardiness are hallmarks. A reputation for tenderness is largely unfounded, a myth generated by Victorians who grew them in pots. They relish a free-range existence and adore sunshine. Their noble verticality and dense orbs of blue – azure, lapis, indigo, sapphire or cobalt – grace and enrich our summer borders like no other plant.

HEIGHT/SPREAD 75cm x 50cm.
ORIGINS South Africa; this cultivar was bred at my own nursery Marchants Hardy Plants.
CONDITIONS Likes moist, free-draining soil.
SEASON July to October. **GG**

Dianthus carthusianorum

'Carthusianorum' meaning: of the monks of the Carthusian Monastery of Grande Chartreuse near Grenoble, France, is perhaps too site-specific given the endemism of this plant throughout Europe, though for that matter the monks may have had a hand in its wide distribution. Its modest foliage passes for a tuft of grey-green grass for much of the year. The small flowers, borne in clusters on lank stems through summer, are anything but modest, being punchy eruptions in dazzling pink. They appear to hover, insect-like – a flamboyant squadron. This craves lime and sharp drainage.

HEIGHT/SPREAD 60cm x 20cm.
ORIGINS Central and southern Europe.
CONDITIONS Well drained, neutral-alkaline.
SEASON Flowers in summer. **GG**

"The noble verticality and dense orbs of blue – azure, lapis, indigo, sapphire or cobalt – grace and enrich our summer borders like no other plant"

Agapanthus 'Marchants Cobalt Cracker'

Tagetes patula L.

This, the original French marigold, is a far cry from the inverted tutu-like flowers that crowd our parks and brighter gardens. From a spring sowing, the first flowers unfold in June, a cheering red-letter day given the dense velvet-textured, yolk-sized, wallflower-red blooms. The bold yellow petal reverse appears as a piped edge, the whole bringing to mind an Elizabethan garment. Sunshine goads flushes of flower for months, the fresh green, cut foliage providing a harmonious background. In autumn, fluted pods cosset a crop of firm, ripe seeds ready for harvest.

HEIGHT/SPREAD 80cm x 30cm.
ORIGINS *T. patula* grows wild in Mexico and Guatemala.
CONDITIONS Likes well-drained soil.
SEASON Flowers from June through to autumn. **GG**

SHARON PEARSON

SHARON PEARSON

Clematis viticella

Bouncing with health, it's small wonder that breeders have been unable to keep their hands off this southern European clematis, though their brassier achievements stray from the simplicity and elegance inherent in this species. Each purple flower, comprised of four sepals (petals), is held on a long purple pedicel (stalk) which, being 'raked', results in a nodding flower, giving the plant its demure character. Flowering on new growth, it can be pruned annually to 30cm without fear but needs a wired wall or host shrub, to support it.

HEIGHT/SPREAD 2-4m x 1.5m. AGM.
ORIGINS Central and southern Europe, western Asia.
CONDITIONS Likes fertile, well-drained soil.
SEASON Flowers from midsummer to autumn. **GG**

Datisca cannabina

False hemp is well documented as a dye plant, all parts being used to produce a yellowish stain (*Datiscetin*). Turkish Nomads still use it. Its emergence in gardens has been relatively slow, perhaps on account of its subtle, wild-ish look. A clumping herbaceous perennial, it makes a striking textural collage of greens, combining tall, arching stems clothed with attractive, cannabis-like foliage and conspicuous, drooping tassels of persistent, tiny flowers (male or female). A cool plant for the hot days of high summer.

HEIGHT/SPREAD 2.5m x 1.8m.
ORIGINS Eastern Mediterranean, central and eastern Asia.
CONDITIONS Likes moist, well-drained soil.
SEASON Clusters of small flowers in July and August. **GG**

SHARON PEARSON

Places to visit

Graham Gough chooses places to see good collections of plants, including National Plant Collections.

Dick and Lorna Fulcher grow dozens of different agapanthus, and have held a National Collection since 1997, in their small garden and nursery, **Pine Cottage,** overlooking the Taw valley in rural mid Devon. Fourways, Eggesford, Devon EX18 7QZ. Open most of the year, but phone before visiting. Tel 01769 580076. www. pcplants.co.uk

Agapanthus sp.

Steven Hickman grows a huge collection of agapanthus at **Hoyland Plant Centre** in Yorkshire. It is not open to the public, but you can see, and buy, plants from the collection at the major garden shows – there's a list on the nursery's website at www. somethingforthe garden.co.uk
The National Collection of kniphofia – red hot pokers – grows among 20 acres of

Agapanthus 'White Heaven'

Sidalcea 'Elsie Heugh'

There is something comfortingly old-fashioned about sidalceas. They were plants that were grown with sweet williams and picked in bunches for the parlour. I like this one best of all for its satiny, pale pink flowers. The fringed petals and tissue-paper texture of the flowers suggest a delicacy that can lighten-up planting schemes of more robust perennials. The pink colour of the flower seems to change depending on its neighbour: planted among the dark stems of *Salvia nemorosa* 'Caradonna', the flowers seem tinged with purple; next to a clump of white corncockle, they fade to pale pink.

HEIGHT/SPREAD 80cm x 40cm. AGM.
ORIGINS Garden hybrid.
CONDITIONS Light, fertile soil in full sun.
SEASON July. **JH**

RACHEL WARNE

SHARON PEARSON

Tilia henryana

Named after its discoverer Augustine Henry, Henry's lime was introduced in 1901 by EH Wilson from central China. In Asia it makes an exceptionally large tree, 25m-plus high. Uncommon and slow in cultivation, however, it makes a handsome small tree or large shrub, though prone to wind damage when young, so shelter is prerequisite. The leaves emerge a downy grey and expand richly copper-tinted, unfurling to reveal characteristic toothed margins. The striking foliage is matched by the astonishing scent of autumn flowers, a cloying mixture of honey and mothballs.

HEIGHT/SPREAD Slow growing, but will eventually reach 25m x 25m.
ORIGINS West Hubei, China.
CONDITIONS Likes moist, well-drained soil.
SEASON Scented flowers in later summer and early autumn. **GG**

Veronicastrum virginicum 'Erica'

German plantsman Ernst Pagels' patience, tutored eye and vision gave rise to an embarrassment of new plants. This selection subscribes typically to important criteria: its wispy flower spires and small leaves have a deft lightness, yet its growth is dense. There's a synthesis of colour in foliage and flower; its vigour is acceptable and its compact nature makes it exceptional among veronicastrums, and a blessing for space-deprived gardeners. (Pictured here with an unusually short Joe Pye weed, *Eupatorium purpureum* subsp. *maculatum* 'Ankum's August'.)

HEIGHT/SPREAD 1m.
ORIGINS A cultivated form of a North American species.
CONDITIONS Any soil type.
SEASON Flowers July to August. **GG**

SHARON PEARSON

gardens at **Barton Manor**, which is open a few times a year for charity. Whippingham, East Cowes, Isle of Wight PO32 6LB. Tel 01983 292835.

The collection of *Clematis viticella* at **Longstock Park Nursery** is displayed on a 100m-long archway. Longstock, Hampshire SO20 6EH. Open most days. Tel 01264 810894, www. longstocknursery.co.uk

SARAH CUTTLE

Kniphofia 'Ice Queen'

Richard and Irene Hodson grow more than 200 *C. viticella* cultivars among old-fashioned roses and perennials in their one-acre garden. **Hawthornes Nursery**, Marsh Road, Hesketh Bank, Lancs PR4 6XT. Open seasonally for groups by appointment only, with the occasional open day held in aid of charity. Tel 01772 812379, www. hawthornes-nursery.co.uk

JASON INGRAM

Clematis viticella 'Maria Cornelia'

Aconitum 'Stainless Steel'

The steely grey-blue flowers have a faint ghostly quality in the low light of early evening. The beautiful dense spikes also make a fine cut flower prized by florists. In borders at home, we plant them to emerge between clumps of *Miscanthus sinensis* 'Morning Light' where the silver variegated grass effectively hides their untidy lower foliage – a common trait of aconitums. *Aconitum* contains toxins which can be absorbed through skin so prolonged exposure could be harmful. Wear gloves to handle plants and flowers.

HEIGHT/SPREAD 100cm x 35cm.

ORIGINS From a Dutch introduction of hybrid origin.

CONDITIONS Fertile, moisture-retentive soil in sun or light shade.

SEASON June to July. **CM**

Heliopsis helianthoides var. scabra 'Summer Nights'

This plant's name aptly conjures up its dramatic contrast of golden flowers and burgundy stems. When first seen in the perennial trials gardens at Hermannshof in Germany, we made a note to add this to our nursery's palette. Plants tend to grow rather tall, and early season pruning makes little impression. We resolved the problem by constructing hazel-twig frameworks through which the plants strain upwards, yet stay invisibly supported. Deadheading will prolong the flowering display.

HEIGHT/SPREAD 175cm x 50cm.

ORIGINS Heliopsis are native to open prairies and scrubs of the USA and Mexico.

CONDITIONS Most fertile garden loams that have moisture retention.

SEASON June to September. **CM**

"The bold yellow petal reverse appears as a piped edge, the whole bringing to mind an Elizabethan garment. Sunshine goads flushes of flower for months, the fresh green, cut foliage providing a harmonious background"

Tagetes patula 'Linnaeus'

Agastache 'Painted Lady'

Had I been offered a plant described as 'a marriage of vivid pink and orange flowers', I might have declined gracefully. In this case, I'm very glad I took up the gift, since the colour combination is glorious, proving that colour harmony is simply a matter of proportion. Slender elongated spikes of peppermint scented flowers are upbeat but not gaudy. They make a fine display all summer long, and miraculously tone with either pink or orange spectrums. A good choice for a summer pot where they will thrive in full sun and demand very little in the way of watering or deadheading.

HEIGHT/SPREAD 70cm x 30cm.

ORIGINS A selection of *Agastache mexicana* from hot, dry climates of southern North America.

CONDITIONS Likes free-draining warm soils. Protect from winter wet.

SEASON Early June to September. **CM**

Aesculus parviflora

A medium to large shrub with a suckering habit that makes ultimate size indications difficult. It is perhaps best as a specimen in an open grass area where its invasive tendencies can be curtailed by mowing (although it grows as a large shrub, unlike most *Aesculus* which are grown into full standard trees). In early summer, branches have an abundance of slender upright flower panicles. Peering into the throat of each flower reveals protuberant red anthers and pretty pink filaments. Juvenile foliage is attractively bronzed, later maturing to mid green before finally achieving an attractive autumnal yellow.

HEIGHT/SPREAD Up to 3m x 3m. AGM.
ORIGINS North America.
CONDITIONS Likes fertile and moisture-retentive soil.
SEASON July to August. **CM**

Phlox paniculata 'Reddish Hesperis'

Summer wouldn't be the same without the classic peppery sweet smell of *Phlox paniculata*. There are dozens of good forms and colours from which to choose, but I encourage you to try this one. 'Reddish Hesperis' is tall in stature, but with finer elegant flower heads comprising lavender-pink blooms, each with a central flash of white. Their smaller scale is more easily blended with other plants in a border while their resistance to mildew earns them another star point.

HEIGHT/SPREAD 100cm-120cm.
ORIGINS Species native to Eastern USA.
CONDITIONS Free-draining loamy soils with good organic content.
SEASON July to August. **CM**

Eryngium amethystinum

This plant steals in on the scene about now. Having quietly grown up through adjacent foliage almost unnoticed, it ripens in the sunlight to a magnificent blue and demands attention. Each flower resembles an intricate Elizabethan ruff, a veritable pollen magnet to bees and butterflies. The stiff and spiny structure is defensive, while ensuring the plant needs no artificial corsetry to stand. Best kept in lean soils to curb ultimate height and to aid their vertical stability.

HEIGHT/SPREAD 60cm x 30cm.
ORIGINS From Italy, Sicily and the Balkans.
CONDITIONS Well-drained loam from mildly alkaline to acidic.
SEASON Best colour from June to August, though the structure endures longer. **CM**

Places to visit

Chris Marchant shares some of her favourite gardens and other places to see plants at their best.

To see massed herbaceous perennials in creative arrangements, visit the pleasure gardens at **Trentham**, Staffordshire, which have been revived by a strong design team – Piet Oudolf, Tom Stuart-Smith and Dominic Cole. Gardens include formal Italian, new perennial, a wildflower meadow and woodlands. There is also a garden centre

Trentham Gardens in Staffordshire.

and a cafe. Trentham Gardens, Stone Road, Trentham, Stoke-on-Trent, Staffordshire ST4 8AX. Open most days. Tel 01782 646646, www.trenthamgardens.co.uk

Contemporary planting on a smaller scale can be seen at **Lady Farm** near Bristol in 12 acres of contrasting garden areas. Each has a strong emphasis on plant communities. A

Acanthus mollis (Latifolius Group) 'Rue Ledan'

There is a classic elegance to the *Acanthus*, its scrolling foliage a feature detail on early Corinthian columns. This form has excellent vigour and rigidity, sporting fine turgid flower spikes of ghostly white. Stems stand for many weeks without staking, and can often endure late into autumn frosts to provide the garden with winter structure and valuable bird food. A reliable mainstay in a prominent north-facing border where dignified green architecture is required.

HEIGHT/SPREAD 100cm-120cm x 60cm.
ORIGINS Species native to Europe. This form originated in a garden in N France.
CONDITIONS Most well-drained garden loam, benefiting from an early spring mulch of leaf mould.
SEASON July to October. **CM**

Kniphofia 'Tawny King'

The drama of kniphofia flowers is fleeting, so choose one with an impressive display. Flower spikes of 'Tawny King' are a brilliant graduation of light orange to gold, fading slowly to creamy buff. Flowers are plentiful, provided the crowns are not overshadowed by neighbouring plants. Teamed with the deep blue spikes of *Nepeta grandiflora* they speak of sunny days and scorching temperatures – even if the British summer is sometimes rather slow to oblige.

HEIGHT/SPREAD 90cm x 40cm. AGM.
ORIGINS Species originate mainly in the mountains and upland grasslands of South Africa.
CONDITIONS Deep, fertile soil in full sun, benefiting from spring and autumn mulch in order to retain moisture.
SEASON June to July. **CM**

Verbascum 'Spica'

The biennial verbascums are invaluable for their rapid introduction of grand scale to juvenile borders. This soft ivory is easily worked into any colour scheme, but I particularly like it among tall blue salvias. Rosettes of giant felted green leaves will perform stoic weed suppression. Since the seeds last for many years in the soil, take care to remove some before ripening, or you will quickly have a verbascum forest. The caterpillars of the mullein moth (*Cucullia verbasci*) can be a problem; pick off or spray to control their ravages.

HEIGHT/SPREAD 2-3m x 50cm.
ORIGINS Native to eastern Europe and Turkey.
CONDITIONS Most well-drained garden loams, including heavy clay.
SEASON June to July. **CM**

steppe garden was created from a difficult mound of subsoil from an old tennis court. A prairie garden looks magnificent from July to December with tall grasses, *Eupatorium* and *Helenium*. There is also a formal cottage garden planted with white tulips. Lady Farm, Chelwood, Bristol BS39 4NN. This private garden is open certain days from July to October. For group visits phone the owner Judy Pearce on 01761 490770. www.ladyfarm.com

The Hannah Peschar Sculpture Garden is a ten-acre sculpture gallery but with the character of a private garden. Exhibits are displayed within the extensive grounds of the house and gallery, set off by broad-leaved plants and mature trees. Contemporary artworks are

The prairie garden at Lady Farm, Chelwood, near Bristol.

for sale, and commissions are undertaken, under the guidance of owner-curator Hannah Peschar and landscape designer Anthony Paul. Each spring brings a new exhibition. Black and White Cottage, Standon Lane, Ockley, Surrey RH5 5QR. Seasonal opening. Tel 01306 627269, www.hannahpeschar sculpture.com

Late Summer

The long lazy days will last a while longer and these gorgeous plants will make the most of your garden while the sun shines. High summer is the time for drama: tall perennials and vivid splashes of colour will keep your borders looking vibrant

Rudbeckia triloba

In this rudbeckia, flowers have golden petals clustered around a chocolate brown cone. The sheer number of blooms can make things top-heavy so grow through hazel cages, which disappear beneath foliage and flower. The golden floral display remains radiant well into November.

HEIGHT/SPREAD **120cm x 65cm.** AGM.*
ORIGINS **North America**
CONDITIONS **Any well-drained loam.**
SEASON **September-November. CM**

Clematis 'Pangbourne Pink'

There is a quirkiness to the way the sepals of this plant twist about that always makes me smile. The flowers themselves dangle from the end of stems that grow above the foliage so it seems as though they are peeping out above the plant. This is a herbaceous clematis that will not climb. It is best left to scramble over the ground or through other plants. Although not much used in Britain as a cut flower, clematis lasts a long time in a vase. Because of its long flower stem this one is particularly suitable for cutting.

HEIGHT/SPREAD **80cm x 50cm.** AGM.

ORIGINS **Selection of *C. integrifolia* 'Rosea'.**

CONDITIONS **Sun or part shade and well drained.**

SEASON **July to September.** JH

Rudbeckia laciniata 'Herbstonne'

By the time we get to midsummer the tall, macho perennials are beginning to make themselves known. They often have coarse foliage and few flowers. *Rudbeckia laciniata* 'Herbstonne' is a low fountain of elegant leaves that have a slightly blue sheen, making them attractive in their own right. The slender stems start to grow rapidly in late July and by August they have branched out and are topped with daisy-like flowers that are typical of the genus. When the flowers are fully open the petals droop down, leaving the cone to point skywards.
HEIGHT/SPREAD 2m x 90cm. AGM.
ORIGINS Garden hybrid of a North American species.
CONDITIONS Prefers heavy, moist soil in sun or part shade.
SEASON July to September. **JH**

Althaea cannabina

When a plant is this good you wonder why it has only been widely grown in the last decade. It has the diaphanous quality of *Verbena bonariensis* but with narrower and taller stems, with masses of one-inch diameter flowers all the way up. Don't stake it. Despite its height it doesn't need it and you will lose the dramatic movement it makes in the breeze. It has a deep tap-root so doesn't grow well in pots. Nursery specimens always look unpromising but soon take off once they are in the ground.
HEIGHT/SPREAD 2.5m x 1m.
ORIGINS From southern and central Europe to the Caucasus.
CONDITIONS Sunny and well drained.
SEASON Flowers July to September. **JH**

"There is a quirkiness to the way the sepals twist about that always makes me smile. The flowers themselves dangle from the end of stems that grow above the foliage so it seems as though they are peeping out above the plant"

Clematis 'Pangbourne Pink'

*The Royal Horticultural Society's Award of Garden Merit (AGM) helps gardeners make informed choices about plants. It indicates that the plant is recommended by the RHS.

Cephalaria balansae

For years I grew this plant's big brother, *Cephalaria gigantea*. I liked its tall, airy stems and scabious-like flowers. Then, in the Bagatelle gardens in Paris, I came across *C. balansae* (then known as *C. dipsacoides*): it is shorter, has finer foliage and paler, cream-coloured flowers. It is a far superior plant. So out came *C. gigantea* and in went my new discovery. I was pleased to find that it self-seeds far less than *C. gigantea* and that bees and insects love the flowers. Mine is in a border but I have recently seen it dotted through a wildflower meadow where it looked very handsome.

HEIGHT/SPREAD 1.5m x 1m.
ORIGINS Western and central Asia.
CONDITIONS Sun and well-drained soil.
SEASON Flowers from the end of July until October. **JH**

Salvia greggii 'Icing Sugar'

All the *Salvia greggii* cultivars flower over a long period. Although there is never a mass of flowers they continue throughout summer. Dozens of new forms are being introduced at the moment. I like this one for the complementary colours of its dark pink and pale pink flowers. Lots of claims are made about the hardiness of this plant but given they have not survived the past two winters, take cuttings at the end of the summer, or treat them as an annual and buy new plants each year.

HEIGHT/SPREAD 50cm x 40cm.
ORIGINS Garden hybrid.
CONDITIONS Sun or part shade, best in well-drained soil.
SEASON Flowers from June until the end of September. **JH**

Lobelia x speciosa 'Tania'

The perennial lobelias have a reputation for being weedy plants that keel over with the first chill of winter. Not this one. I find that it is a strong grower, vigorous and hardy. It needs to be kept dry in the winter, so on clay soils dig lots of grit into the area before you plant. Strong colours like this are not for the faint-hearted and can be difficult to place. Mine are growing among the bright foliage of the feather reed grass *Calamagrostis* x *acutiflora* 'Avalanche', which makes the flowers seem even brighter. I've seen it looking good with pink cleomes and with a purple-leaved *Physocarpus*.

HEIGHT/SPREAD 1m x 50cm.
ORIGINS Garden hybrid.
CONDITIONS Likes a sunny place, in moist but well-drained soil.
SEASON July to September. **JH**

Places to visit

John Hoyland recommends places to visit for a good display of plants in late summer.

If you want to see salvias in all their variety, head to **Great Comp** garden, near Sevenoaks in Kent. The curator, William Dyson, is a *Salvia* expert and the garden is full of ideas about how to incorporate salvias into planting schemes. There is even a salvias border. The nursery is crammed with salvias, including many that are difficult to find elsewhere

Great Comp

and ones bred at Great Comp. Comp Lane, Platt, Borough Green, near Sevenoaks, Kent TN15 8QS. Seasonal opening. Tel 01732 885094, www. greatcompgarden.co.uk

Stoneacre is a Kentish yeoman's house that dates back to the 15th century. The surrounding gardens have been sympathetically designed and planted to provide a romantic setting for

Sanguisorba officinalis 'Red Thunder'

My soil is too well drained to give most sanguisorbas the moist conditions they prefer. This one, though, copes well with my dry soil, although it never reaches the height of 2m that it will in rich, damp soil. The flower stems branch in every direction, with a dark red, tightly-packed flower on the end of each. The plant is so floriferous that you get a cloud of red flowers through to the end of September. I am growing my plants with *Panicum virgatum* 'Squaw', which at the end of summer starts to turn the same deep red as the flowers of the *Sanguisorba*.

HEIGHT/SPREAD 2m x 60cm.
ORIGINS Seedling selected by Piet Oudolf from plants collected in Korea.
CONDITIONS Sunny and moist.
SEASON July to September. **JH**

x *Alcalthaea suffrutescens* 'Parkallee'

During the summer the tall spires of hollyhocks are an irresistible sight. Don't look too closely, though, because the foliage is usually covered in rust. Fortunately it is now possible to have flowers as beguiling as hollyhocks but with minimal rust. *Alcalthaea* has a shrubby appearance with grey, velvety leaves and creamy-apricot flowers. It is a beautiful combination that continues right through to the autumn. Usually said to need lots of sunshine, mine are thriving in shade under conifers.

HEIGHT/SPREAD 2m x 1m.
ORIGINS A hybrid between two members of the mallow family, Althaea and Alcea.
CONDITIONS Sun or shade in well-drained soil. Avoid soil that stays wet in winter.
SEASON Late July to end of October. **JH**

Clematis florida var. *normalis* Pistachio (='Evirida')

At the height of summer it is rare to find plants that have a fresh look about them, but the green-tinged flowers of this clematis seem to cool the air on hot, bright days. At the centre of the flower is a tight pom-pom of short stamens with pink-grey anthers, which enhance the brightness of the sepals. As the season progresses the green tinge becomes more pronounced, so that by the autumn the flowers are living up to their name. It was bred to be both a garden plant and one that will grow in a conservatory.

HEIGHT/SPREAD 1m x 50cm.
ORIGINS Introduced by clematis breeder Raymond Evison.
CONDITIONS Sun and well-drained soil.
SEASON July to the end of September (or much later if grown under glass). **JH**

the house. The property is owned by the National Trust and its former tenants were clothes designers renowned for their fresh and exciting planting schemes. Otham, Maidstone, Kent ME15 8RS. Seasonal opening. Tel 01622 863247, www.nationaltrust.org.uk
Close to both these gardens is **Sissinghurst Castle**, one of the country's most important 20th-century gardens, created by Vita Sackville-West and Harold Nicolson. It is divided into small garden rooms, each with a different character of colour or theme – a riot of colour. Its famous white garden has been hugely influential. As we search for new gardening experiences it is easy to overlook venerable old gardens like Sissinghurst.

Sissinghurst Castle

It is true that the garden is often too crowded and its maintenance perhaps a little institutional, but it also true that the spirit of the place rings through, and much of its planting remains inspiring. Biddenden Road, near Cranbrook, Kent TN17 2AB. Seasonal opening. Tel 01580 710700, www.nationaltrust.org.uk

Miscanthus sinensis 'Malepartus'

The most comprehensive breeding work on miscanthus was by German nurseryman Ernst Pagels in the 1970-80s. He wanted to produce cultivars to flower reliably in the shortish summers of northern Europe. This is one of the results. The bronze flower spikes, are the most spectacular of the genus. I have clumps of this behind the white-flowered *Acanthus mollis* (Latifolius Group) 'Rue Ledan' – see page 57 – and the two look splendid. Too many *Miscanthus sinensis* cultivars have been introduced. This is head and shoulders above the rest.

HEIGHT/SPREAD 2.2m x 1.2m.
ORIGINS Bred by nurseryman Ernst Pagels.
CONDITIONS Needs rich, well-drained soil in full sun.
SEASON Flowers August to October. **JH**

Anisodontea capensis

If you visit the Western Cape province of South Africa in late spring or early summer you can't fail to be struck by this pretty shrub. You can hardly see the thin wiry stems because the whole plant is covered with small pink flowers. In the UK, *Anisondontea capensis* rarely survives its first winter so never reaches the height of two metres that you can see in the wild in South Africa. I take cuttings of my plants in late summer and overwinter them, both cuttings and parent plant, in a cold greenhouse. You can see from the shape of the flowers that it is a relative of the hollyhock.

HEIGHT/SPREAD 60cm x 60cm.
ORIGINS South Africa.
CONDITIONS Sunny, well-drained soil.
SEASON August to October. **JH**

"The contrast between the sombre foliage and the bright flowers makes all the dark-leafed dahlias exuberant plants. Dahlia 'Moonfire', with its grenadine and orange flowers, is particularly jovial"

Dahlia 'Moonfire'

Dahlia 'Moonfire'

The contrast between the sombre foliage and the bright flowers makes all the dark-leafed dahlias exuberant plants. *Dahlia* 'Moonfire', with its grenadine and orange flowers, is particularly jovial. It was bred in the Netherlands in 2001, leading a pack of new introductions of dark-leaved dahlias that hoped to emulate the popularity of *D.* 'Bishop of Llandaff'. There are now so many that there is hardly a bishopric in Britain, real or imagined, that doesn't have a dahlia named after it. Dahlia 'Moonfire' is much shorter than the bishops but none of them make such a sparkling impact.

HEIGHT/SPREAD **75cm x 50cm.** AGM.
ORIGINS **Bred in the Netherlands.**
CONDITIONS **Full sun or part-shade with free-draining soil.**
SEASON **July to October.** JH

Salvia 'Phyllis' Fancy'

Lots of imposing salvia hybrids have been appearing lately but this one has to be the most dramatic. The whole plant is two metres tall with 30cm long flower spikes. The individual flowers are an eye-catching combination of pale lavender petals surrounded by a purple calyx. The colour of the stem and of calyces darkens as the temperature drops. There are reports that is has survived to as low as -10°C, but I don't believe it will cope with the damp and cold of even a mild British winter, so take cuttings and keep mature plants in the greenhouse over winter.

HEIGHT/SPREAD 2m x 1.5m.
ORIGINS Santa Cruz Arboretum, California.
CONDITIONS Well-drained soil in full sun.
SEASON August until first frosts. **JH**

RACHEL WARNE

RACHEL WARNE

Dahlia 'Arabian Night'

However many varieties of dahlia I try, there is a core group that I always grow and this is one of them. The full-bodied flowers of 'Arabian Night' are a vibrant wine-red colour that seem to respond to the slightest change in the light. Sometimes the petals appear crimson and at others they are almost black. Traditionally dahlias tubers are lifted in the autumn, dried and stored in a cool place during the winter. I plant my tubers deeply (about 20cm) and leave them in the ground. I lose fewer plants this way than by lifting them.

HEIGHT/SPREAD 1.2m x 50cm.
ORIGINS Garden hybrid.
CONDITIONS Likes rich and well-drained soil in full sun.
SEASON August to October. **JH**

Mathiasella bupleuroides 'Green Dream'

This monotypic genus (it has just one species) was only described in 1954 and named after Dr Mildred Mathias, a Californian taxonomist. Like all its relatives in the carrot family, *Apiaceae*, its flowers have exquisite form. This is no exception, with dreamy, soft green bracted heads and black flowers. After several months the heads mature to pink. The foliage is grey-green and presents nicely after a few years when it has clumped-up.

HEIGHT/SPREAD 60-120cm x 60cm (after three years).
ORIGINS Northeast Mexico.
CONDITIONS Effective in close-up, so plant where it will be seen. Seems tolerant of most conditions except wet soils.
SEASON Spring to autumn. **BB**

TORIE CHUGG

Places to visit

John Hoyland recommends places to visit for a good display of plants in late summer.

Aylett Nurseries in Hertfordshire, now a large garden centre, began as a specialist dahlia grower. The nursery still produces hundreds of varieties of dahlias and maintains its collection in fields near the garden centre. The dahlia field is open to view from August until the first frosts. For two weekends in September when the plants are at their best, a

BIBLIO PHOTOGRAPHY / ALAMY

Chenies Manor

special exhibit of cut dahlias is staged at the nurseries along with other gardening subjects. North Orbital Road, St Albans, Hertfordshire AL2 1DH. Garden centre open most days. Tel 01727 822255, www.aylettnurseries.co.uk

To see dahlias growing in a garden, head for **Chenies Manor** at Rickmansworth. The owner Elizabeth MacLeod Matthews uses exuberant

Lilium 'Robina'

Even the dying stems of this have caused comment, in November. It's the size – a full 3m. The flowers are huge and superlatively scented. Like all lilies, it has its problems. I approach lily beetles with one hand, then catch them with the other as they drop off. Even so-called lime-tolerant kinds react to my highly alkaline clay, so I excavate a large hole and fill it with acid compost, which, to my surprise, lasts for years. This is the most heady plant I grow. Play to the audience and put it where it can be seen from the road. It can even hold its own against shrubs.

HEIGHT/SPREAD 3m x 45cm.
ORIGINS A complicated hybrid with a long lineage of Asian origin.
CONDITIONS Plant in fertile acid loam and full sun.
SEASON Mid to late summer. **BB**

TORIE CHUGG

RACHEL WARNE

Fuchsia 'Whiteknights Blush'

The daintiness of this fuchsia's flowers makes it far more endearing than the brash and blowsy hybrids that are usually associated with the genus. Pale pink and slender, the flowers first start to appear in July, but the plant is at its most floriferous in September. When I first grew this fuchsia I took cuttings to overwinter in the greenhouse, believing that the plants that I had left in the garden would be dead by the spring. However I was wrong, and my plants have survived outside for the last seven years, which have included a couple of quite atrocious winters.

HEIGHT/SPREAD 60cm x 50cm.
ORIGINS Garden hybrid.
CONDITIONS Well-drained soil and full sun.
SEASON July to October. **JH**

Sedum telephium 'Xenox'

Many sedums have been looking good since the spring but they are only now beginning to flower. A lot of them will become top heavy with flowers and will flop over, leaving an ugly mess in the middle of the border. 'Xenox' is a recent introduction from the Netherlands and it is a strong-stemmed and compact plant that keeps its domed shape even when smothered in flowers. Early in the year the foliage is grey-green and covered with a dusky-blue sheen. As the summer progresses this darkens until by September it is a shiny burgundy colour. The flowers are soft pink and will last through October.

HEIGHT/SPREAD 30cm x 30cm. AGM.
ORIGINS Garden hybrid.
CONDITIONS Sun and well-drained soil.
SEASON September and October. **JH**

RACHEL WARNE

groups of dahlias among perennials and shrubs throughout the garden. The dahlias are generally on show from July to the first frosts. The Manor House, Chenies, Buckinghamshire WD3 6ER. Seasonal opening. Tel 01494 762888, www.cheniesmanorhouse.co.uk

Late summer is the time for dahlias and at **Anglesey Abbey**, in Cambridgeshire,

there is a dedicated dahlia garden that was established in the 1940s by Lord Fairhaven. When the National Trust took over the property in 1966, the Trust's garden adviser, Graham Stuart Thomas, opined that dahlias were not worthy plants for a great garden and should be removed. Fortunately the gardeners ignored him and thanks to them we can see

Dahlias at Anglesey Abbey

DAVID LEVENSON / NTPL

the garden as it is today. Many of the plants such as the delightful red-flowered *Dahlia* 'Madame Simone Stappers' are old varieties that could have been lost were it not for Anglesey Abbey's gardeners. Quay Road, Lode, Cambridge, Cambridgeshire CB25 9EJ. Seasonal opening. Tel 01223 810080, www.nationaltrust.org.uk

Dahlia 'Pumpkin Pie'

If you are really nice to most plants, they respond by dying.
Dahlias don't. This one was selected in 2004 from a whole
Dutch field full of new seedlings by coach loads of women
visitors (honestly). The whole package of foliage, flower,
stems and even the pollen in the middle is cooked to
perfection. It's always worth risking leaving your dahlias in
the ground overwinter. Some risk does come from the
winter cold but a far greater risk comes from snails that
graze off the emerging shoots like asparagus in the late
spring. Defend them.

HEIGHT/SPREAD **30cm x 30cm.**

ORIGINS **Selected in the Netherlands.**

CONDITIONS **Prefers moist, well-drained soil, but will
grow in poor soils too. Likes full sun.**

SEASON **High summer to autumn. BB**

Leucanthemum x *superbum* 'Cream Crochet'

Thank God it inherited only *some* of its characteristics from its mother, *L.* 'Sonnenschein', the first yellow(ish) shasta daisy. 'Sonnenschein' has two faults – the flowers fade to the colour of old urine and the flowers stems are contorted. In contrast, 'Cream Crochet' has wonderful semi-double flowers that stay the same pure, pale cream as they fade. Its father ('TE Killin') gave it a soldierly, upright habit and extra petals. The best shasta daisies have good dark green foliage – and this is one of them.

HEIGHT/SPREAD 1m x 50cm.
ORIGINS Its ancestors are a combination of a wild double oxeye daisy from a Norfolk railway embankment and an Iberian daisy.
CONDITIONS Ordinary soil.
SEASON Mid to late summer. **BB**

Apios Americana

This is one of those plants you can't believe you've never seen before because it has so many advantages. It's a herbaceous twining climber with fresh new growth every season; it's utterly hardy; it has lusty blooms in a tired season and edible tubers (one thing I haven't eaten, but it's a traditional food of Native Americans). Its perfume of sweet violets is unexpected. It reached Europe as a garden plant in 1597 and was even trialled as a substitute for potatoes in the Irish potato famine. Why doesn't everyone grow it? Plant beneath a sunny wall, where it will grow through other climbers that tend to be bare at the base, such as honeysuckle and jasmine.

HEIGHT/SPREAD 3m x 1m.
ORIGINS North America.
CONDITIONS Any soil is fine.
SEASON August and early September. **BB**

"If you are really nice to most plants, they respond by dying. Dahlias don't. The whole package of foliage, flower, stems and even the pollen in the middle is cooked to perfection"

Dahlia 'Pumpkin Pie'

Helenium 'Sahin's Early Flowerer'

I was with Kees Sahin on a visit to his trial ground in the Netherlands on 1 November 1996 when he kicked this plant with the toe of his shoe and told me to take some. I admit I am quarrelsome so the response, "Why?" is no surprise. "Because it's in flower now and it has been since early June." I can add that it is shorter than many heleniums (a good thing) and that the flowers are long-lasting when picked and get brighter as the nights cool. Kees was a seedsman and plant breeder, gregarious, sharp-witted and the best plantsman I've known. He died in 2006.

HEIGHT/SPREAD 90cm x 50cm. AGM.
ORIGINS Midwest USA and into Canada.
CONDITIONS Sunny places, avoid unimproved clay soils.
SEASON Midsummer to late autumn. **BB**

Hydrangea macrophylla 'Merveille Sanguine'

The plantsman John May took my son and me to see an overgrown specimen of this at Logan Botanic Garden in Dumfries and Galloway. It had cobalt-blue flowers unlike anything I had seen before. Twelve years later I got it from a French nurseryman. In my growing conditions the colour is more attractive than at Logan. The leaves have a deep red cast that intensifies in late summer and the flowers are an equally deep red. I hadn't thought about the name until it was pointed out that it roughly translates as 'Bloody Marvellous'. That's that, then!

HEIGHT/SPREAD 1.4m x 1m.
ORIGINS Japan.
CONDITIONS Shade or half-shade with reliably moist soil that's not too limey.
SEASON Late summer and autumn. **BB**

Polystichum setiferum 'Pulcherrimum Bevis'

Here we have another example of tissue culture in laboratories upsetting people who are put out when a formerly rare and desirable plant becomes cheaper and more commonly available. The ends of the fronds are fetchingly curved, giving the whole plant tremendous grace and making it the plant of choice for most fern cognoscenti.

HEIGHT/SPREAD Eventually grows to 1.1m x 1.3m. AGM.
ORIGINS English form of native soft shield fern found on a Devon roadside in 1876.
CONDITIONS Plant in shady places. It prefers open soil but isn't fussy.
SEASON Evergreen fronds fabulous at any time of the year but excel in late summer and autumn. **BB**

Places to visit

Bob Brown suggests gardens to visit that are at their best in late summer.

The Cotswold Wildlife Park combines the best late summer landscape planting in the savanna and prairie style with zebra and rhinoceros. Catch the park with thunderstorms around and you'll be convinced that you are in Kenya. It also has an impressive series of exotic/tender gardens. Near Burford, Oxfordshire OX18 4JP. Open most days,

The Cotswold Wildlife Park

Tel 01993 823006, www.cotswoldwildlifepark.co.uk
The name **Stone House Cottage Garden** is a misnomer, for 'cottage garden' does not convey the grandeur of James Arbuthnott's walls, gazeboes and follies that divide this former walled kitchen garden into a series of garden rooms with diverse habitats. These, combined with Louisa's

Pennisetum alopecuroides 'Black Beauty'

Aptly named 'fountain grass' on account of its autumn cascade of busby-like flowers produced from tight clumps, this is native to high-rainfall areas in eastern Asia. In gardens its performance is weather-dependent and thus slightly unpredictable, given the increasing volatility of our climate. A hearty, moisture-retentive soil and average rainfall will encourage it to flower freely. A variable species in size and colour, this form with suave black purple flowers is one of the smartest, and in the picture sophisticatedly partners a rich *Persicaria* in a long autumn duet.

HEIGHT/SPREAD 60-150cm x 60-120cm.
ORIGINS The species grows wild from eastern Asia to Japan and Australia.
CONDITIONS Needs fertile and moist soil.
SEASON Summer and autumn. **GG**

SHARON PEARSON

TORIE GHUGG

Geranium Rozanne (= 'Gerwat')

I am not easily seduced by geraniums. There are far too many and people are far too keen. They all look the same – weedy looking growth and pink flowers. Not this. The flowers are lilac, get bluer as the nights cool down and there are touches of red round the foliage and in the stems. It dies back to the same growing point each winter but in a season can cover at least a metre sideways starting into growth and flower (the two are concurrent) often as late as June for me.

HEIGHT/SPREAD 35cm x 1m. AGM.
ORIGINS Found in the garden of Donald and Rozanne Waterer in Kilve, Somerset.
CONDITIONS Mine is in dry semi-shade but it's pretty adaptable, and thrives in any soil.
SEASON Midsummer to late autumn. **BB**

Dahlia 'Murdoch'

This is an old cultivar and my favourite. It was brought to me in 1993 by one of the old school of dahlia-growers to propagate and keep in cultivation. I'm always willing to do my bit for conservation but was taken aback when it produced its remarkably clear, deep-red flowers that put what I had considered other clear red flowers into the shade. The flowers have burnished golden bracts, which help the effect.

HEIGHT/SPREAD 1m x 70cm.
ORIGINS Bred in Burnley, Lancashire in 1944. Its ancestors are Mexican.
CONDITIONS Like all good dahlias it responds to good cultivation and care; it prefers moist, well-drained, soil, but will grow in poor soils too. Full sun.
SEASON High summer to autumn. **BB**

TORIE GHUGG

talented planting and choice of the most interesting plants, makes this a garden that has to be visited. It is full of unusual and rare plants, many of which can be bought in the adjoining nursery. Stone House, near Kidderminster, Worcestershire DY10 4BG. Seasonal opening. Tel 01562 69902, www.shcn.co.uk
Upton House Gardens
teeter on the northern edge of

JENNY LILLY /GAP

Stone House Cottage and Gardens

the Cotswolds, with borders so blowsy I associate them with that melting moment when sleep comes. They are especially good in late August. Go on a warm day to explore its terraces, borders, kitchen garden and tranquil water garden. Near Banbury, Warwickshire OX15 6HT. Seasonal opening. Tel 01295 670266, www.nationaltrust.org.uk

NTPL/STEVEN ROBSON /ALAMY

Upton House and Gardens

Stachys officinalis 'Hummelo'

A frequent host to clouds of butterflies, this is a versatile and tolerant plant, which will flower in spite of thin and poor soil conditions. Tightly formed rosy purple blooms, not dissimilar to our native early purple orchid, will stand tall for many weeks, their finished height dependent on moisture levels and nutrient. I have used plants with equal success in the midst of a low-maintenance shrub framework and on the edge of an informal damp meadow. Try partnering with forms of *Origanum laevigatum* to draw even more insects.

HEIGHT/SPREAD 50cm x 50cm.
ORIGINS Europe and north Africa.
CONDITIONS Prefers a well-drained warm soil, but is tolerant of low nutrient soils.
SEASON June to August, perhaps a second flush September to October. **CM**

Euphorbia seguieriana subsp. *niciciana*

Good or bad, the front row of any border makes a lasting impression, which is why you need well-behaved subjects for this high-profile role. This *Euphorbia* erupts each spring with a nest of slender stems bearing needled grey-green foliage. Characteristic flower bracts of acid yellow offer strident contrast to any neighbouring plant and form organised mounded hummocks. Plants need only a brisk trim over in late October to ensure a shapely and plentiful display the following year.

HEIGHT/SPREAD 40cm x 45cm.
ORIGINS Found in many places, from Europe to northwestern China.
CONDITIONS Demands well-drained light soil in full sun.
SEASON May to September. **CM**

"Fragile crinkled, papery flowers, the size of a saucer, enfold golden stamens, which belie its iron constitution. In appearance, one cannot help but think of a host of fried eggs"

Romneya coulteri

Sedum 'José Aubergine'

The trouble-free habits of most *Sedum spectabile* justify the energy invested in breeding new colourful varieties. *Sedum* 'Matrona' introduced us to exciting beetroot-toned foliage, but had a tendency to get too tall for some spaces. Not so the newer Sedum 'José Aubergine', which boasts the same colours, but retains a slightly more stocky and manageable habit. I team this with *Penstemon* 'Andenken an Friedrich Hahn' and *Salvia verticillata* 'Smouldering Torches' in a south-facing border to make sure the garden doesn't go down with a whimper in August.
HEIGHT/SPREAD **50cm x 45cm.**
ORIGINS **Species occurs across Russia and China to Japan.**
CONDITIONS **Well-drained garden loam in sun or part shade.**
SEASON **Flowers form in August and stand into December. CM**

Lathyrus latifolius 'Blushing Bride'

This combines beauty and persistence. Its sister is the ordinary magenta-pink sweet pea that flourishes over railway embankments, which says a lot about its ability to survive neglect. This one is more subtle and it's one of summer's delights to see the clusters of sculpted flowers against a blue sky. One of mine scrambles over the dark leaves of *Trachelospermum jasminoides*, which throws the flowers into prominence. The flowers, though unscented, are good for picking.

HEIGHT/SPREAD 2.5m x 1m.

ORIGINS Europe.

CONDITIONS It climbs with tendrils, so it needs a bush, a wall or another climber to cling to as it re-grows each year.

SEASON Mid to late summer. **BB**

Teucrium hircanicum 'Paradise Delight'

Standing over an expansive planting of this *Teucrium* in flower brings to mind a host of firework sparklers. Each stem supports an elongated lime green spike, opening to rosy purple flowers from the base upwards. I turn to this plant in massed border plantings to provide structure and texture into the winter months. Spurning stakes, and demanding no special pruning, the effect is both impressive and easy. Be sure to leave spent flower heads standing through winter frosts to give overwintering garden birds a pit-stop meal.

HEIGHT/SPREAD 55cm x 45cm.

ORIGINS Northern Europe.

CONDITIONS Most fertile garden loams.

SEASON July to October. **CM**

Aster x herveyi (previously Aster macrophyllus 'Twilight')

Asters, in their many guises, extend our enjoyment of flowering through the shortening days to autumn. This one in particular gives maximum pleasure with minimal effort. Tolerant of sun or light shade, it used to be known as *Aster macrophyllus* 'Twilight', and it certainly lives up to that name. Strong upright stems require no staking, holding aloft flat-headed clusters of single daisies in azure blue. The plant is equally at home in formal arrangement or casual disarray, and makes a worthy contribution to the late-summer garden.

HEIGHT/SPREAD 65cm x 35cm.

ORIGINS North America.

CONDITIONS Any good garden loam.

SEASON August to early October. **CM**

Places to visit

Chris Marchant shares some of her favourite gardens and other places to see plants at their best.

As the season ripens, I am drawn to gardens that boast a productive orchard. **Lytes Cary Manor** in Somerset was formerly the home of herbalist Henry Lyte, and still houses his 16th-century plant directory 'Lytes Herbal'. The Grade II listed house and Arts and Craft-style garden were rescued from dereliction in the early 20th century by Sir Walter Jenner. Imposing

Step back in time in the gardens at Lytes Cary Manor

long herbaceous borders have been replanted to an original Graham Stuart Thomas design, and good examples of Elizabethan-style topiary and outdoor rooms lead you through the space. Step into the secreted old orchards where medlars and quince trees stand decked with forming fruit and you can almost believe that time has spun back 400 years. Lytes

Romneya coulteri

It may take a year or two, but once established, this plant has remarkable vigour (you will need to edit to required size). So much so, I have watched it emerge from under the foundations of a wall to sprout triumphant on the sunnier side. Fragile crinkled, papery flowers, the size of a saucer, enfold golden stamens, which belie its iron constitution. In appearance, one cannot help but think of a host of fried eggs. There is a perfect partnership between it and a fine-walled garden, but even if you have just a small section of brick, it will be all the finer for the addition of this plant.

HEIGHT/SPREAD Can reach 2m x 2m if unchecked. AGM.
ORIGINS Native of southern California.
CONDITIONS Well-drained neutral to alkaline loam.
SEASON July to August. **CM**

Kniphofia 'Green Jade'

Raised and introduced by Beth Chatto, this plant really rises to the occasion when borders begin to look rather dry and forlorn. Its elegant profile has great architectural strength, requiring no staking if nutrient levels are kept lean. The effect offers interesting contrast when threaded through some of the ripening mid-height grasses, such as *Panicum virgatum*, or *Calamagrostis brachytricha*. The pale green colour, fading to creamy white is incredibly versatile, and can be used to form a cooler bridge between the many fiery reds and oranges of late summer.

HEIGHT/SPREAD 120cm x 45cm.
ORIGINS Species found in mountains and upland grasslands of South Africa.
CONDITIONS Well-drained soil in full sun.
SEASON From the end of August through to September. **CM**

Agapanthus praecox

There is some confusion over the naming of this plant, which was originally sold to us as *Agapanthus africanus*. Agapanthus experts have advised it was more correctly a *praecox* type. Either way, it is best used in a pot and moved into a double-skinned polytunnel for winter protection from the end of October until May. Small price to pay for the glorious display of blue spherical flowers, held above broad strappy foliage, and replaced later by beautifully structured seed heads in butter yellow.

HEIGHT/SPREAD 100cm x 50cm.
ORIGINS Southern Africa.
CONDITIONS Needs a moisture-retentive, nutrient-rich soil.
SEASON Flowers in July with attractive seed heads through into September. **CM**

Cary Manor, Charlton Mackrell, Somerton, Somerset TA11 7HU. Seasonal opening. Tel 01458 224471, www.nationaltrust.org.uk.
There are more orchards at **Waterperry Gardens** in Oxfordshire, where lines of old-fashioned fruiting varieties peel off into the distance. Come back in autumn for Apple Weekend, when you can bring up to three examples of garden fruit for variety identification. Waterperry Gardens, near Wheatley, Oxon OX33 1JZ. Tel 01844 339254, www. waterperrygardens.co.uk
Once considered one of the most innovative gardens of the 19th century, **Biddulph Grange** in Staffordshire has been restored by the National Trust. The 15-acre garden boasts many features

Enjoy the glorious dahlia walk at Biddulph Grange

(including a kitchen garden, woodland walk, lake and summer bedding displays) but of particular merit at this point in the season is the splendid dahlia walk, which is brimming with more than 600 dahlias. Grange Road, Biddulph, Staffordshire ST8 7SD. Open most days. Tel 01782 517999, www.nationaltrust.org.uk

Persicaria amplexicaulis Taurus (='Blotau')

The range of *Persicaria amplexicaulis* now available to plant lovers is potentially bewildering. But if you choose to measure performance against reliability, flower colour and longevity this one comes pretty near the top in the rankings. It was a chance seedling, identified by Alan Bloom at Bressingham in Norfolk. Vibrant rose-madder flowers are marginally shorter than the species, and swollen in girth to impressive effect. Individual flowers sport a tuft of electric blue stamens. Extended flowering is a bonus.

HEIGHT/SPREAD **100cm x 70cm.**

ORIGINS **Persicarias originate in Northern temperate regions.**

CONDITIONS **Prefers a humus-rich, moisture-retentive soil, but copes with less.**

SEASON **July to October. CM**

Vernonia arkansana 'Mammuth'

Ephemeral detail can ebb and flow but every successful border needs a framework of reliable structure plants that endure. Here, stems the thickness of a man's finger reach up nearly two metres without need for support. When September brings golden daisies and wheaten grasses, the flattened heads of *Vernonia*, each having myriad small composite flowers, stand out in purple splendour. It serves well as fine marker points in formal planting; and is equally successful mixed with a range of meadow grasses in wilder spaces.

HEIGHT/SPREAD 175cm x 80cm.
ORIGINS Native to eastern North America.
CONDITIONS Most well-drained loams in full sun.
SEASON August to October, with good structure beyond. **CM**

Miscanthus sinensis 'Emmanuel Lepage'

Originally a gift from French nurseryman Monsieur Lepage, this was a chance seedling in his stock beds in the Loire. He selected it for good form and colour and named it after his father. *Miscanthus sinensis* cultivars contribute reliable height, colour and movement from August to February. This one is particularly valuable, retaining fresh green foliage pretty much until Christmas. Prolific flowering stems unfurl to display gently arching plumes with a silken sheen. It is a fine partner to *Eupatorium* cultivars.

HEIGHT/SPREAD 200cm x 100cm.
ORIGINS *Miscanthus sinensis* species originate in Southeast Asia.
CONDITIONS Most moisture-retentive garden loams.
SEASON August to November. **CM**

> *"Front edges of borders, like a pretty smile, get noticed. This slender, upright aster is eminently suitable for a front row position"*
>
> *Aster sedifolius* 'Nanus'

Aster sedifolius 'Nanus'

Front edges of borders, like a pretty smile, get noticed and unsightly dark spaces in either can be alarming. This slender upright aster is eminently suitable for a front row position, ensuring colour into autumn. Reliable and mildew resistant, it requires little attention. Branched stems support plentiful composite flowers, opening to lavender blue in August. A bonus is the attractive wheaten structure which remains well after flowers fade. 'Nanus' was first seen on the stony banks of Lake Baikal in Siberia, where it withstands harsh winter temperatures.

HEIGHT/SPREAD 40cm x 30cm.
ORIGINS South and east central Europe to northern Asia.
CONDITIONS Well-drained loam in an open aspect.
SEASON August to September. **CM**

Sedum telephium subsp. ruprechtii

Not every sedum is pink; I like the mellow buff tones of these flowers as a complement to the dark purples and blues of late summer. Newly opened blooms on this more sprawling plant are a creamy yellow, against a glaucous foliage. Long summer days bring on a darkening of flower tone. By the first frosts, flowers have acquired a light biscuit bronze, and foliage is marked with attractive pink flushes. Mixed with *Euphorbia polychroma* and *Stipa calamagrostis* in a gravel scree, the cameo endures from May to October.

HEIGHT/SPREAD 40cm x 40cm.
ORIGINS Widely distributed throughout northern temperate regions.
CONDITIONS Free-draining garden loam, tolerant of lean nutrient conditions.
SEASON July to September. **CM**

Eryngium ebracteatum

At first glance you might easily mistake this plant for a *Sanguisorba*. Wiry stems bear multiple flowers in warm claret tones, so redolent of the *Sanguisorba* family. But the fine upright habit and slender saw-edged leaves confirm a tolerance of more arid conditions. Both plants contribute a strong architectural statement in scree or gravel planting. Position where the flower heads can be silhouetted against a late summer sky, and protect from winter wet to preserve the plant for future years. Collect some seed anyway, for added insurance against unpredictable British winters.

HEIGHT/SPREAD 100cm x 45cm.
ORIGINS South America.
CONDITIONS Free-draining alkaline to neutral soils.
SEASON July to September. **CM**

Places to visit

Chris Marchant names some favourite walled gardens that look impressive this month.

The Walled Garden at Scampston Hall has a bold contemporary design from renowned Dutch plantsman Piet Oudolf, leaning heavily on herbaceous plants and grasses for colour and texture. In September the massed grass parterres turn warm golden brown, contrasting with the rich colour palette of late summer perennials. Scampston Hall,

Scampston Hall walled garden planted by Piet Oudolf

Malton, North Yorkshire YO17 8NG. www.scampston.co.uk
There is a special charm to all walled gardens, but the historic kitchen garden at **Audley End** in Essex is magnificent. Just under 100m long, it has a range of fruit, vegetables and flowers much of which is available to buy through the shop. It is managed for English Heritage by Garden Organic. Audley

Persicaria virginiana var. *filiformis*

As other plants begin to wane, this *Persicaria* justifies its place in the garden. Principally grown for the velvet textured foliage, its emerald leaves are symmetrically marked with an attractive chocolate-brown blotch. Wine-red stems repeatedly branch into an airy structure, the terminal wisp of stem so slender it is scarcely visible. Until, that is, tiny flower buds open to reveal a perfect pinpoint of vivid scarlet.

HEIGHT/SPREAD 65-80cm x 50cm.
ORIGINS Species introduced from America by John Tradescant the younger.
CONDITIONS Prefers a moisture-retentive soil in light shade and protected from harsh winds.
SEASON Foliage from June, flowers from September. **CM**

Crocosmia x *crocosmiiflora* 'Star of the East'

This plant presents the perfect example of how a glorious orange flower lift the spirits and brightens a fading border. Coral buds open to star-shaped blooms up to 10cm across, with masses of sword-like green foliage. A triumphant marriage of beauty and resilience and awarded an RHS Award of Garden Merit. 'Star of the East' is an Earlham hybrid raised by George Davison who thereafter turned to apple breeding, believing the form could never be surpassed. A confident commendation!

HEIGHT/SPREAD 70cm x 35cm. AGM.
ORIGINS Crocosmia species originated in South Africa.
CONDITIONS Moisture-retentive loam, ideally not drying excessively in summer.
SEASON Flowers from late August to the end of September. **CM**

Verbena bonariensis 'Lollipop'

We still sell more *Verbena bonariensis* than any other plant, but you may not have sampled this diminuitive version and I urge you to investigate. Flattened congested clusters of vibrant purple flowers are held aloft on rigid stems. Longevity of flowering display contributes greatly to its value in feature planters and high profile beds. Used with *Erigeron karvinskianus* and *Molinia caerulea* subsp. *caerulea* 'Moorhexe', a large planting trough provided a billowing show of colour and texture from June to November, with almost no watering required.

HEIGHT/SPREAD 60cm x 30cm.
ORIGINS Species originates from Buenos Aires, after which it is named.
CONDITIONS Tolerates well-drained thin and lean soils in sunny aspect.
SEASON June until first frosts. **CM**

End, Saffron Walden, Essex CB11 4JF. Seasonal opening. Tel 01799 522842, www.english-heritage.org.uk
The Inner Temple Garden in London is not quite walled, but it is an enclosed space, which became a formal garden after it was gifted to the Society of the Inner Temple by James I in 1608. A new dynamic phase began recently with the arrival of

Andrea Brunsendorf as head gardener. Her creative plantsmanship has introduced new successional planting with emphasis on late summer colour. The ancient avenue of plane trees is thrown into colourful relief by a carpet of 13,000 Liriope muscari – a sight to behold when flowering in September. Inner Temple Garden, Crown Office Row, Inner Temple,

Audley End House and Gardens in Essex

London EC4 7HL. www.innertemple.org.uk
A West Midlands park hosts a National Collection of rudbeckias, at their best in late summer. It's in a Victorian walled garden at Stevens Park, Wollescote Road, Stourbridge DY9 7JG. Open most days. Tel 01384 815589, www.friendsofwollescote park.co.uk

Sedum 'Red Cauli'

This was selected by Graham Marchant at Marchant's Nursery. Its principal fault for nurserymen is that pot and plant are never in the same place. Pick up what you think is a plant and a plant 60cm away comes up. This waywardness doesn't matter in the garden and almost nothing else could provide the incredible tomato-red colouring. This may look like it is an artificially enhanced photograph but truly the plant is this colour. Tasty!

HEIGHT/SPREAD 20cm x 50cm (allow for the sprawl). AGM.

ORIGINS Its parentage might be complicated but owes much to British native orpine *Sedum telephium* (which grows throughout the northern hemisphere).

CONDITIONS Does well in sun or half sun.

SEASON August to September. **BB**

TORIE CHUGG

SHARON PEARSON

Caryopteris x clandonensis 'Kew Blue'

West Clandon in Surrey is immortalised in the name of this splendid autumn-flowering shrub, being the place of its discovery in the 1930s. A hybrid of *Caryopteris incana* and *C. mongholica*, it is unperturbed by soil pH. Its timing is perfect, flowering when most plants are on the wane. The blue flowers, uncommon at this season, are enhanced by the cooler prevailing weather. *C.* x *clandonensis* 'Kew Blue' stands the test of time and can hold its own among modern cultivars.

HEIGHT/SPREAD 1m x 1.5m.

ORIGINS *Caryopteris* grows wild in the Himalayas and western Asia.

CONDITIONS Light, moist and well-drained soil with sharp drainage and sunshine.

SEASON Flowers late summer and early autumn. **GG**

Aster 'Little Carlow'

My commonest response to diseased plants is to walk away. Take Michaelmas daisies and mildew. It doesn't kill the plants but leaves shrivelled foliage and poor flowers. The commonest control is to spray systemic fungicide once a month from April onwards. Life is too short – and I'd never remember. Not every aster gets mildew and it's easier to plant these than to struggle to keep the others looking good. Many of them are also not so prone to sudden violent infections by mildew, like most kinds of Michaelmas daisies. My favourite is 'Little Carlow', which has the RHS Award of Garden Merit (AGM). The flowers are so blue it hurts the eyes – yet it's not a strident blue.

HEIGHT/SPREAD **1m x 45cm.** AGM.

ORIGINS **North American origins but it was bred in Devizes in the 1930s.**

CONDITIONS **Needs sun or half sun, in any soil that is not waterlogged.**

SEASON **August to October.** BB

TORIE CHUGG

"As a purple mantle clouds the leaves, white fruits swell – a congregation of doll's eyes casting a communal startled gaze at the brilliant autumn light"

Cornus alba 'Sibirica'

Euphorbia griffithii 'Dixter'

Some plants have one great aria; others perform all season long. From the moment the red-flushed stems appear in early spring to its crescendo of autumn colour, *E. griffithii* takes centre-stage. Its stems and leaves are suffused with maroon and its flower heads are bright orange. It sends suckers out, but if you don't want it where it pops up, just pull it out before it becomes established. The late Christopher Lloyd spotted this cultivar, which has redder stems than the species, in a batch of plants from Washfield Nursery in Kent.

HEIGHT/SPREAD 60cm x 1m. AGM.
ORIGINS *E. griffithii* is native to the Himalayas.
CONDITIONS Sun or semi-shade, in well-drained soil.
SEASON Red stems in spring; flowers May to September; yellow autumn foliage. **JH**

RACHEL WARNE

SHARON PEARSON

Cornus alba 'Sibirica'

Better known for its dramatic red stems in winter, the Siberian dogwood takes a humbler back seat in summer with its cloak of ribbed, large green leaves. It's hardly grown for its flowers, of which there tend to be few because most gardeners cut it to the ground in spring to encourage colourful stems the following winter. The white posy-like flower clusters it does produce largely go unnoticed, but not by industrious bees. As a purple mantle clouds the leaves, their labour is rewarded – white fruits, a congregation of doll's eyes casting a communal startled gaze at the brilliant autumn light.

HEIGHT/SPREAD 2m x 2m (unpruned). AGM.
ORIGINS Siberia, China.
CONDITIONS Any; prefers moist soils.
SEASON White berries in late summer; red foliage in autumn; red stems in winter. **GG**

Aster 'Pixie Red Eye'

It's going to sound like crowing but I always sleep soundly on planes. This doesn't mean that I don't understand how inappropriate this plant name is. Amazingly it was bred in Israel to be a cut flower. It is mildew-free, hides its dead flowers like a *Bouvardia*, grows into compact mounds and the wonderful rich plum colour is not marred by an aster's normal yellow eye. It responds to careful cultivation in good, well-drained soil. A desirable cultivar. Enlivens borders of maturing *Geranium endressii* and decaying penstemons.

HEIGHT/SPREAD 60cm x 45cm.
ORIGINS This was bred in Israel from North American species.
CONDITIONS Sun or half sun, but needs soil that's not waterlogged.
SEASON September to October. **BB**

TORIE CHUGG

Places to visit

Bob Brown names some of his favourite gardens and other places to see plants at their best.

Old Court Nurseries, and the Picton Garden, Colwall near Malvern, which specialises in Michaelmas daises, is a must for September and the first half of October. Nowhere else will you see such a wide range of Michaelmas daisies so incredibly well kept. Take a notebook and a camera and plan to destroy and replace some of the also-ran plants in your garden (dare I mention

Old Court Nurseries

JASON INGRAM / GAP PHOTOS

ubiquitous *Geranium* x *oxonianum* 'Hollywood' and *Centaurea montana*) with some zestful asters. If you have space remember to plant some simply for cutting. Old Court Nurseries, Colwall, Malvern, Worcestershire WR13 6QE. Seasonal opening. Tel 01684 540416, www. autumnasters.co.uk

Newby Hall has 25 acres of award winning gardens.

Helianthus 'Carine'

Chris Ghyselen understands his plants more than the average garden designer. Part of his style seems to be to design with plants, which, if you were to walk away, would still be there in 50 years – really tough plants. *Helianthus* 'Carine' was a seedling selected by him from *H.* 'Lemon Queen' – which itself is well known as a reliable, ultra-tough, late summer and autumn perennial daisy with soft yellow flowers. 'Carine' has even softer yellow flowers and it's shorter. It's set for a great future. My wife wants Chris to design her next garden.

HEIGHT/SPREAD 1.5m x 50cm.
ORIGINS Selected in Belgium, from North American species.
CONDITIONS Sun or half sun, not dry soils.
SEASON Flowers from late summer to early autumn. **BB**

Panicum virgatum 'Northwind'

Switch grasses, once synonymous with the vast prairies of America, have long proved themselves as garden plants, in many shapes and sizes. Their use in American gardens is a relatively recent development, and led to many handsome introductions. *Panicum virgatum* 'Northwind' is no exception. Its tough, broad, sage-green leaves stand bolt upright and are said to resist hurricane-force winds. In the garden, its pillar-like habit makes the perfect punctuation. Its flowers may be modest, but it has a terrific autumnal leaf-palette of ambers, golds and yellows.

HEIGHT/SPREAD 2m x 1m.
ORIGINS North and Central America.
CONDITIONS Thrives in most soils.
SEASON Upright 'column' of foliage in summer, colouring well in autumn. **GG**

Persicaria orientalis

An annual with attitude (it is listed in the *Global Compendium of Weeds*) this glorious Asian knotweed presents few problems for the adventurous gardener who needs only confidence, a stake to support its looming 2.2m tall stems, and a hoe to shave off unwanted spring seedlings. In rich soil these develop rapidly (quicker still when sown under glass), achieving their dizzy height by August. The first terminal flowers dangle, bobbing bait to insects and ridiculously disproportionate to the huge, lush leaves below. They gain momentum as the weeks pass, climaxing in a rich pink shower of tiny, fade-proof flowers.

HEIGHT/SPREAD 2.2m x 80cm.
ORIGINS East and Southeast Asia, Australia
CONDITIONS Moist and fertile.
SEASON Late summer, early autumn. **GG**

Highlights include one of Europe's longest double herbaceous borders as well as a large collection of rare shrubs, including cornus. The autumn garden is at its best from August onwards, and has late summer flowering herbaceous plants. Ripon, North Yorks HG4 5AE. Seasonal opening. Tel 0845 450 4068, www.newbyhallandgardens.com

Bressingham Gardens display perennials, grasses, shrubs, trees, conifers, ferns and bulbs in distinct areas over several acres. In high summer the Foggy Bottom garden, designed by Adrian Bloom, mixes perennials and grasses in a colourful border. Diss, Norfolk IP22 2AB. Seasonal opening. Tel 01379 686903, www.bressinghamgardens.com

Sussex Prairies

Looking good at this time of year is **Sussex Prairies,** a six-acre display garden. It is a sea of herbaceous perennials and grasses in free-flowing combinations, planted in large drifts. Morlands Farm, Wheatsheaf Road, Henfield, West Sussex, BN5 9AT. Seasonal opening. Tel 01273 495902, www.sussexprairies.co.uk

Crataegus x *lavalleei* 'Carrierei'

I pass this in two churchyards on my journey to the nursery. One of the trees is backed by a stained-glass window from which coloured light floods out. The combination is breathtaking. Orange in July can look uncomfortable. Orange in winter is astonishing and welcome.

HEIGHT/SPREAD **3-4m x 3-4m.** AGM.*

ORIGINS **This is a hybrid between *Crataegus crus-galli* from Eastern North America and *C. pubescens* f. *stipulacea* from Mexico, discovered in the Segrez Arboretum near Paris in about 1880.**

CONDITIONS **Tolerates any soil, in full sun.**

SEASON **At its best from November to February. BB**

Autumn & Winter

Cold weather arrives, but there's still plenty of interest in the garden. These plants will ensure winter borders are filled with colour, form and scent, as late-flowering perennials give way to flame-coloured leaves, vivid berries and shapely seedheads

Cercis canadensis 'Forest Pansy'

This large shrub or small tree has many merits, but growing in a balanced symmetrical form would not seem to be one of them. Our own specimen was a house-warming gift from friends and our appreciation of the kind gesture increases year on year as the tree develops. Branches often turn upon themselves at crazy angles, and the creaking structure now demands strategic propped support to mitigate collapse. But the gold and aubergine tints on its leaves and the sight of laden branches backlit against a pale blue sky are exquisite. This RHS Award of Garden Merit plant should be a feature of more gardens.

HEIGHT/SPREAD **Up to 6m tall with an 8m spread.** AGM.

ORIGINS **Native to Eastern North America.**

CONDITIONS **Most well-drained soils with good humus content.**

SEASON **Tiny crimson flowers in May, with show-stopping leaf colour from September onwards. CM**

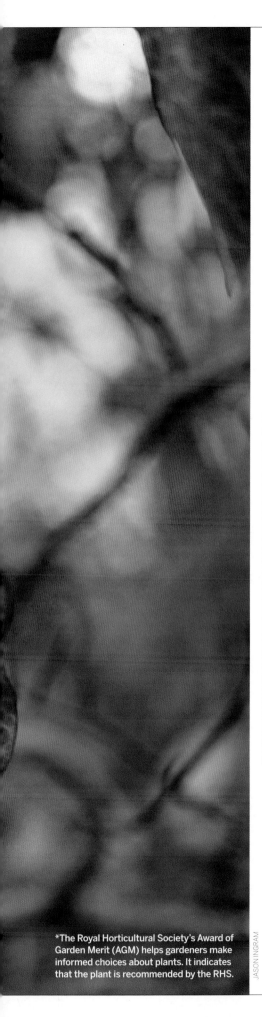

Miscanthus sinensis 'Krater'

This shorter *Miscanthus* is particularly useful in the front or middle rank of a deep border, where I find it provides a strong visual anchor during the colder months without obscuring other shapely forms. The narrow green blades have a pronounced white mid-rib; gently arching flower stems rise taller to support a host of chestnut-brown flower panicles during September and October. By November the foliage has mellowed to a warm biscuit brown, and plumes have attained a silvery sheen. This scene is set until you choose to cut back, which we do in February, to await the new season's growth.

HEIGHT/SPREAD 150cm x 60cm.
ORIGINS Species originates in Eastern Asia.
CONDITIONS Most fertile garden loams.
SEASON September to November. **CM**

Ageratina altissima 'Braunlaub'

Striking, high-colour plants sometimes need a foil and I love the way this plant can be offered up to such a wide range of classics to achieve the necessary bridge between strong or strident colours. Helenium, rudbeckia, aster and crocosmia are eased into a harmonious group when partnered with *Ageratina*. Groups of this plant growing on the nursery will regularly attract clouds of butterflies – a good reason to include them in any garden. *Ageratina* was previously grouped with *Eupatorium* in its classification, and the characteristics are very similar.

HEIGHT/SPREAD 100cm x 60cm.
ORIGINS North America.
CONDITIONS Free-draining garden loam.
SEASON Late August to October. **CM**

"Autumn foliage turns gradually to orange, presenting bright crimson before falling. At once, the tree is left naked but for the brilliant red fruits which adorn the boughs, like a blushing Salome resplendent in nought but jewels"

Crataegus persimilis 'Prunifolia'

Crataegus persimilis 'Prunifolia'

I sense a whiff of eastern exoticism about this small tree, spectacular in its autumn foliage, which turns gradually to orange, presenting bright crimson before falling. At once, the tree is left naked, but for the brilliant red fruits which adorn the boughs, like a blushing Salome resplendent in nought but jewels. Earliest cultivation can be traced back to the 18th century when it occurred as a hybrid of two North American species. A beautiful small tree, but with significant thorns, so position it with care. This is an RHS Award of Garden Merit plant.

HEIGHT/SPREAD 6m x 4-5m. AGM.
ORIGINS North American parentage.
CONDITIONS Most fertile garden loam.
SEASON Flowers from May to June, with fruits from September to November. **CM**

Cladrastis kentukea

Cladrastis comes from the Greek, translating as 'brittle shoot'. One of the *Leguminosae* family, its fragrant flowers appear in late spring in extravagant pendulous clusters, followed by slim, elongated pods. Sadly, the flowers are rare in Britain, requiring prolonged early warmth to ripen the buds, but it has other merits and even our cooler climate will gradually progress the fresh green leaves to golden pinnate foliage in autumn. At this point, the tree shines a warming cast over a chilly autumnal garden. It can be successfully pollarded to keep the profile in check if required.

HEIGHT/SPREAD Up to 20m x 7m.
ORIGINS Eastern USA.
CONDITIONS Likes moisture-retentive soil.
SEASON Attractive foliage September to October. **CM**

Cyclamen mirabile

All cyclamen are good but this looks better than most and has received an Award of Garden Meris from the RHS. The foliage has an amazing flush of pink for about two months in the autumn. Beneath, the leaves look crystalline and sparkle in strong light. They settle down to being pewter and green with a purple reverse, by which time the delicate pink flowers have stolen the show. I keep mine in a cold greenhouse but bring them inside if extreme frost threatens. For a hardy plant, try *Cyclamen hederifolium*, which is naturalised in Britain.

HEIGHT/SPREAD 12cm x 12cm. AGM.
ORIGINS Mild southwest Turkey.
CONDITIONS Grow as a specimen in pots where it can be protected against frosts.
SEASON Foliage September to March, flowers September to October. **BB**

Places to visit

Chris Marchant shares some of her favourite places to see plants at their best.

Great Fosters in Surrey began life as a royal hunting lodge in 1550. Now it is a luxury hotel set in 50 acres of gardens and parkland forming a glorious marriage of ancient and modern. Over the past century, the gardens have been restored, extended and enhanced by various skilled practitioners. A recent and exciting addition is the sensuously

Curved grass amphitheatre, designed by the landscape architect Kim Wilkie

curved grass amphitheatre, designed by the landscape architect Kim Wilkie. Set as the focal point at the end of a Lime Avenue, its simplicity of form and balance of scale are brilliant. Non-resident guests are able to book afternoon tea at the hotel. Great Fosters, Stroude Road, Egham, Surrey TW20 9UR. Tel 01784 433822, www.greatfosters.co.uk

Rosa x *odorata* 'Bengal Crimson'

"Don't you know it?" Helen Dillon asked me in her Dublin garden in 1996. "Have some cuttings." They all rooted. Subsequently I discovered this plant's strange habits. It produces masses of flowers about five times a year, with a few in between. In the shelter of the Chelsea Physic Garden the November and February bloomings are unbelievable. If planted against a wall it goes straight up and does its thing at the top. The foliage, branching and flowers are airy and delicate. Few thorns.

HEIGHT/SPREAD 2m x 1.75m or taller against a wall.
ORIGINS China.
CONDITIONS A sunny spot. I grow it in gravely loam and clay equally well.
SEASON March to December. **BB**

JASON INGRAM

Malus x *zumi* 'Golden Hornet'

A neat pyramidal habit and tolerance of light pollution makes this tree ideal for smaller urban gardens where it serves well as a pollinator for other *Malus* cultivars. Buds are pink, opening to fragrant white blossom. Small groups, arranged in groves, make an enchanting sight, in spring and autumn. Long, slender branches are tested by the abundance of their golden harvest, when amber fruits the size of marbles are an invitation to fieldfares. Awarded an RHS Award of Garden Merit.

HEIGHT/SPREAD 10m x 8m. AGM.
ORIGINS A hybrid between *M. baccata* and *M. sieboldii*.
CONDITIONS Well-drained neutral to alkaline loam.
SEASON Flowers in May, fruits August to November. **CM**

TORIE CHUGG

Allium thunbergii 'Ozawa'

This is a neat plant with cheerful bright purple flowers. The neatness is not so extreme that it's of interest to alpinists but it needs not to be smothered by bossier border plants. Mine grows atop a stone wall where I can defend it against the ingress of *Bergenia* and *Sedum* foliage, and the greyness of the wall sets off the colour well. It seems impervious to early frosts and even early snow. Most alliums bloom in spring or early summer. This brings a breath of spring just when it's needed.

HEIGHT/SPREAD 20cm x 20cm.
ORIGINS Japan and Korea.
CONDITIONS Plant it in pots or borders where it will not be smothered.
SEASON October to December. **BB**

TORIE CHUGG

The magnificent walled estate at **Buscot Park** (20 miles southwest of Oxford) incorporates a Grade II-listed historic park and garden with a beautiful water garden by Harold Peto, set within a wooded glade. More recently, the walled kitchen garden was given a contemporary twist by garden designer Tim Rees including a new pleached avenue of *Ostrya carpinifolia* (hop hornbeam) and a tunnel of *Cercis siliquastrum* (Judas tree). It is a fine example of a gracious family garden, lived in and currently administered by Lord Faringdon on behalf of the National Trust. Seasonal opening. Buscot Park, Faringdon, SN7 8BU. Tel 01367 240786, www. buscot-park.com

On a more intimate scale, I never tire of visiting local

A tall group of echinops in the border at Buscot Park

DAVID NIXON / GAP PHOTOS

woodland for an autumn walk. Planning a visit is easier with the website **www.visitwoods.org.uk**, which tailors suggested places to your postcode, access requirements and particular likes. It features woods owned by a range of trusts and charities and aims to ensure that families spend more time enjoying them.

Aster novae-angliae 'Marina Wolkonsky'

My soil is too light and dry to grow asters well and by this time of year they are leafless stems of mildew. Occasionally I find one that will tolerate my garden's soil or that is too beautiful to pass by. When I first saw this growing in a French garden I was lured by the siren-call of its dark flowers. It breaks all the rules of good gardening to grow something unsuited to the situation but I go weak in the presence of beauty. A deep mulch kept moist during summer mitigates the inappropriate growing conditions.

HEIGHT/SPREAD 1.2m x 50cm.
ORIGINS Garden hybrid of the New England aster, from eastern North America.
CONDITIONS Sunny, open situation in rich moist but well-drained soil.
SEASON September to the first frosts. **JH**

Euonymus alatus 'Compactus'

In most shrubs and trees, the brightness of autumn colours varies from year to year, but the most intensely red leaves are always to be found on this *Euonymus*, known as the winged spindle. Each year there is a magical but melancholic moment when a really hard frost knocks all the leaves off and the bare stems of the shrub sit in a pool of red. Euonymus are often grown for their vivid fruits but while this plant produces small orange berries they are less spectacular than the fruits of other species. For dazzling foliage, this is the one to grow.

HEIGHT/SPREAD 1m x 1m. AGM.
ORIGINS Korea, Japan and parts of China.
CONDITIONS Plant in a sunny spot, with moist but well drained soil.
SEASON October and November. **JH**

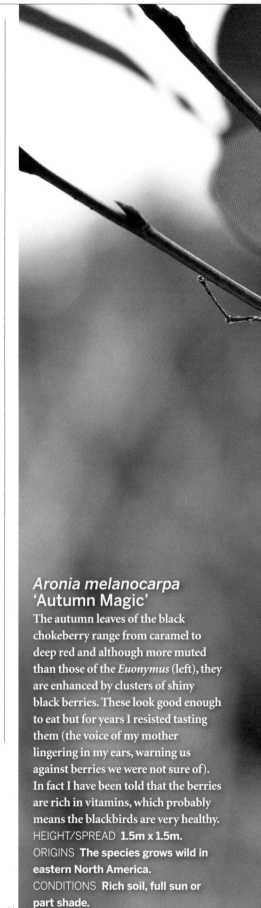

Aronia melanocarpa 'Autumn Magic'

The autumn leaves of the black chokeberry range from caramel to deep red and although more muted than those of the *Euonymus* (left), they are enhanced by clusters of shiny black berries. These look good enough to eat but for years I resisted tasting them (the voice of my mother lingering in my ears, warning us against berries we were not sure of). In fact I have been told that the berries are rich in vitamins, which probably means the blackbirds are very healthy.

HEIGHT/SPREAD **1.5m x 1.5m.**
ORIGINS **The species grows wild in eastern North America.**
CONDITIONS **Rich soil, full sun or part shade.**
SEASON **Spring flowers, with berries and foliage from September to November. JH**

"Each year there is a magical but melancholic moment when a really hard frost knocks all the leaves off and the bare stems of the shrub sit in a pool of red"

Euonymus alatus 'Compactus'

Nerine 'Zeal Giant'

The quality of hardiness in nerines depends on winter dormancy and leafing from spring to autumn (rather than over winter). These characteristics are evident in *Nerine bowdenii* but whatever cultivar you grow, its flowers are samey. The late Terry Jones crossed *N. bowdenii* with the enriched colours of the winter-leafing and tender *N. sarniensis*, aiming for richer colours and hardiness. He famously selected this hardy hybrid, which has huge flowers on long stems that I gather in armfuls for the house.

HEIGHT/SPREAD 75cm x 15cm from a single bulb but clumps up. AGM.
ORIGINS A hybrid of South African species.
CONDITIONS Plant them anywhere (in sun) where they will not be crowded.
SEASON October to November. **BB**

Aster laevis 'White Climax'

This is an old-fashioned invasive Michaelmas daisy. However, it has many good qualities to offset its running habits. It flowers late in the year; frost has little or no effect on the flowers; the foliage is mildew-free and a good deep green; it refuses to die as a plant; it's a fantastic and welcome cut flower (and serves as cut foliage and cut bud earlier); late bees and butterflies love it and the centre of the flower has a lovely greenish hue. In less solid clay than mine it's easy to limit its spread by pulling it up.

HEIGHT/SPREAD 1.5m x 1km.
ORIGINS Northern USA, southern Canada.
CONDITIONS It will spread, but paths hem mine in and shrubs have a similar effect. Tolerates most soils.
SEASON This aster flowers from October to November. **BB**

Salvia 'Waverly'

When I first grew this plant I had a sense that it was going to be disappointing and would end up in the compost. By the middle of September there was no sign of flowers but then, within a two-week period, it had sent up 30cm-long flower spikes that were covered in dark raspberry buds. The flowers are white with just a hint of pink bled through them and are the texture of velour. Waiting was worthwhile: it is a beautiful plant. It won't survive the winter in Britain, so take cuttings or grow it in a frost-free greenhouse or conservatory.

HEIGHT/SPREAD 1.2m x 50cm.
ORIGINS Garden hybrid raised in California.
CONDITIONS Well-drained soil in sun or shade. Needs protection from frost.
SEASON Flowers August to November. **JH**

Places to visit

John Hoyland names some of his favourite gardens and other places to see plants at their best.

The majority of British gardeners have lost the habit of planting perennials and shrubs in the autumn. In Europe in general (and France in particular) the tradition is still strong, and one of France's most important plant fairs coincides with the start of the planting season. Les Journées des Plantes at **Courson**, 35km southwest of Paris, attracts some of the

Les Journées des Plantes, Courson

best nurseries from throughout Europe and takes place each October. Domaine de Courson, 91680 Courson-Monteloup (Essonne). Tel +33 1 64 58 90 12, www.domaine-de courson.fr
Not far from Courson is the **Château of Saint-Jean de Beauregard** where Muriel de Curel has recreated a beautiful flowering potager within a 17th-century walled

Sarcococca hookeriana var. humilis

Hips, berries and seedheads are as important at this time of year as flowers in high summer. Sarcococcas scented the air at the beginning of the year and now they are a mass of berries, which start red and turn black as they ripen. I like the brief period when there are red and black berries on the shrub at the same time. To grow more sarcococcas, try sowing the seed. Just squash a few berries on to the top of a pot of seed compost. They germinate quickly and next year you will have small plants.

HEIGHT/SPREAD 60cm x 60cm.
ORIGINS Western China.
CONDITIONS Well-drained soil in full or partial shade.
SEASON Flowers January to March, berries in October and November. **JH**

Parahebe 'Snow Clouds'

Some early-flowering perennials and shrubs will produce a second display of flowers if the first crop is cut back as soon as it is over. However, anyone who has waited for a second coming of, for example, oriental poppies, will know that claims about a plant's re-flowering habits are often exaggerated. This little treasure, though, really does put on a magnificent display at this time of year, as long as you trim it to remove dead flowers in late May.

HEIGHT/SPREAD 25cm x 25cm.
ORIGINS Parahebes grow wild in Australia, New Zealand and Papua New Guinea.
CONDITIONS Well-drained soil in sun or partial shade.
SEASON May and again September to October. **JH**

Kniphofia rooperi

This is the last poker of the season to flower – and what a finale it makes. There is always a point in September when there is no sign of life among the dense foliage and you think that it is not going to flower. Then fat stems start to push themselves through and within a week they are a metre tall and forming buds. When the flowers open they are slightly larger than a cricket ball and glow an iridescent orange and yellow. Mine are planted among the dark purple flowers of *Aconitum fischeri*, the intense colours of both plants complementing each other.

HEIGHT/SPREAD 1.2m x 80cm. AGM.
ORIGINS Eastern Cape of South Africa.
CONDITIONS Sunny spot, in moist but well-drained soil.
SEASON September to November. **JH**

garden. The park and garden are delightful and absorbing at any time of the year; during autumn the potager is unmissable. Rue du Château, 91940 Saint-Jean de Beauregard. Tel +33 1 60 12 00 01, www.domainstjean beauregard.com

Despite a reduction in government funding, the parks and gardens of Paris still have plenty to offer curious gardeners. **Le Parc de Bagatelle**, situated in the 16th arondissement on the western edge of the city, is one of the four gardens that make up the botanic gardens of Paris. Le Parc de Bagatelle is of the best-maintained and most imaginatively planted public gardens in France. www.french-gardens.com/ gardens/bagatelle.php

Patrick Blanc's mur vegetal'

The narrow streets of Paris were one of the inspirations behind designer Patrick Blanc's **Mur Vegetal** (green wall). One of the best examples is outside the BHV Homme shop on Rue de la Verrerie (4th arrondissement). For a list of locations see the designer's website at www.murvegetalpatrick blanc.com/realisations/

Chasmanthium latifolium

Much is made of the beauty of grasses during the autumn and winter. Pictures of sunlight sparkling on panicles covered with hoar frost are very seductive, but, in fact, the days when we see this are rare. *Chasmanthium*, though, looks attractive during autumn and early winter even without the frost. Diaphanous copper-coloured seedheads are flat and dangle from arched stems. It has a reputation for seeding itself everywhere. My clumps are growing in the top of a low wall and I have not had a problem with unwanted seedlings.

HEIGHT/SPREAD **75cm x 50cm.**
ORIGINS **United States and Mexico.**
CONDITIONS **Well-drained soil.**
SEASON **Autumn and winter. JH**

Viburnum x *bodnantense* 'Dawn'

In the 1930s Charles Lamont of the Edinburgh Botanic Garden crossed *Viburnum farreri* and *V. grandiflorum* but discarded the offspring as being unexceptional. He should have persevered because a few years later the same cross was made at Bodnant Gardens in North Wales and produced this, which has become one of the most widely grown winter-flowering shrubs. The heavily scented flowers appear in November, just as the last of its leaves are falling, and persist through to February or March.

HEIGHT/SPREAD 3m x 2m. AGM.
ORIGINS Bred at Bodnant Gardens, Wales.
CONDITIONS Rich, loamy soil, in full sun or dappled shade.
SEASON Flowers from November through to February. **JH**

Chrysanthemum 'Mei-kyo'

There has been a recent resurgence of interest in hardy chrysanthemums. I've been growing this one in my garden for the past ten years and it came through the wretched winter of 2010, so is probably as hardy as it will ever need to be. The flowers are more demure than many chrysanthemums and in mild weather will last through to Christmas. After a few years the plant can become untidy, with woody stems, so divide it or take cuttings to rejuvenate it. The best time to do either is in the early spring.

HEIGHT/SPREAD 70cm x 70cm.
ORIGINS Garden hybrid of east Asian origin.
CONDITIONS Likes fertile, well-drained soil, situated in full sun.
SEASON October to November or later. **JH**

"For a few fleeting days there are green, red, yellow and mahogany coloured leaves all on the same tree. Eventually they catch up with each other to form a column of deep red and gold – a dazzling sight"

Liquidambar styraciflua

Rhus typhina

This was growing in the nursery when we arrived and my instinct, knowing how it spreads, was to take it out. The job of removing was overlooked, and I've now come to appreciate it more each year. No foliage turns such a bright, fiery red in the autumn. As the weather gets worse the leaves, which drip in long fringes from the branches, become bright orange and yellow. The effect is spectacular, and has saved the shrub from the chop. And getting rid of it would be difficult: it sends thick, strong suckers everywhere. Only grow it if you have plenty of space.

HEIGHT/SPREAD 3m x 3m. AGM.
ORIGINS North America.
CONDITIONS Fertile, well-drained soil in sun or part-shade.
SEASON Wonderful colour in autumn. **JH**

RACHEL WARNE

RACHEL WARNE

Hesperantha coccinea f. alba

The species (formerly *Schizostylis coccinea*) has bright red, bowl-shaped flowers that look as if they belong in a midsummer border. This form has smaller white flowers with narrow petals that create a star-like effect and feel much more at home in the waning weeks of the year. It can be a temperamental plant, particularly in dry soils. To thrive it needs far more moisture than its South African origins might suggest, so mulch regularly with moisture-retaining compost. In mild winters a few tenacious flowers hang on until December, and one year we even had flowers at Christmas.

HEIGHT/SPREAD 30cm x 10cm.
ORIGINS South Africa.
CONDITIONS Rich, moist soil in full sun.
SEASON September to November. **JH**

Dryopteris affinis

As work in the garden slows down there is time during the winter to pause and examine plants that get overlooked during the rest of the year. Ferns tend to play a supporting role during the summer as a foil to more exuberant plants. But on mild winter days when they are illuminated by the low winter sun you can see the beauty of each individual leaf. What during the summer was a green mound becomes, on closer inspection, an intricate tracery of translucent green fronds. This species is evergreen during all but the harshest winters.

HEIGHT/SPREAD Up to 1m x 80cm. AGM.
ORIGINS British native.
CONDITIONS Needs cool, moist soil in dappled shade.
SEASON Year-round interest. **JH**

RACHEL WARNE

Places to visit

John Hoyland names some of his favourite gardens and other places to see plants at their best

Many gardens that are open to the public close down during the winter months but Britain's botanic gardens remain open and, with their balmy glasshouses whose plants take you around the world, are ideal for visits on chilly winter days.

At the **Royal Botanic Garden, Edinburgh** there is always something intriguing and unusual. Early in

Royal Botanic Garden Edinburgh

JOHN PETER PHOTOGRAPHY / ALAMY

November, look out for *Sorbus aff. filipes*, a small tree that has startling bubblegum-pink berries. Within a few weeks they fade to white. Inverleith Row/Arboretum Place, Edinburgh EH3 5LR. Open most days. Tel 0131 248 2909, www.rbge.org.uk

The University of Oxford Botanic garden has its own arboretum six miles south of the city. **The Harcourt**

Malus x robusta 'Red Sentinel'

This crab apple is the one of the best trees for small spaces: it doesn't get too big and has flowers in spring and fruit in autumn. The apples hang in small bunches, like shiny red cherries, but are tough and taste bitter. There are lots of recipes around for using the fruit but I leave them as winter food for the voracious blackbirds. The RSPB recommends crab apples not just because of the fruit but also because the trees are home to more than 90 varieties of insect. I don't know who did the counting and can't vouch for the number, but that's a lot of insects for the birds to eat.

HEIGHT/SPREAD Eventually up to 5m x 5m. AGM.
ORIGINS Garden origin.
CONDITIONS Well-drained soil in full sun.
SEASON Flowers in May, with fruit in September to December. **JH**

Clematis cirrhosa 'Jingle Bells'

A native of several countries that border the Mediterranean, *Clematis cirrhosa* is not always hardy in Britain. Clematis breeders have done a lot of work selecting hardy forms and in the 1990s one of them introduced this cultivar. Its buttermilk-coloured flowers smother the plant through the winter. The dark green glossy foliage provides a perfect background to the flowers. As life is draining out of the rest of the garden, out pop the flowers of this clematis to remind you that the whole cycle will soon begin again.

HEIGHT/SPREAD 35cm x 1m.
ORIGINS Found in the garden of Donald and Rozanne Waterer in Kilve, Somerset.
CONDITIONS Mine is in dry semi-shade but it's pretty adaptable, and thrives in any soil.
SEASON Midsummer to late autumn. **JH**

Liquidambar styraciflua

If I were to design from scratch the perfect tree I would probably come up with *Liquidambar*. In the autumn the leaves seem to change colour one by one so that for a few fleeting days there are green, red, yellow and mahogany coloured leaves all on the same tree. Eventually they catch up with each other to form a column of deep red and gold. It is a dazzling sight. As a bonus the bark on mature trees has a tracery of corky channels. When I lived in France I would enclose *Liquidambar* leaves in letters to friends to show them what they were missing.

HEIGHT/SPREAD Eventually 25m x 12m.
ORIGINS North and Central America.
CONDITIONS Best in rich, moist and slightly acidic soil.
SEASON Amazing in Autumn. **JH**

Arboretum is a magical place at any time of the year but like all arboreta it is an explosion of colour in autumn. The core of the arboretum is a pinetum, which provides an evergreen backdrop to some truly spectacular foliage. Nuneham Courtenay, Oxfordshire OX44 9PX. Seasonal opening. Tel 01865 343501, www.harcourt-arboretum.ox.ac.uk

National Botanic Garden of Wales

Oxford is Britain's oldest botanic garden and the **National Botanic Garden of Wales** is the newest, established in 2000. It is building collections of many genera, including winter-flowering witch hazels, but at this time of year head straight for the Great Glasshouse. Here you can see plants from the Western Cape area of South Africa as well as a display of plants from southwest Australia. Designed by Sir Norman Foster, it is a relaxing place to linger, especially on a cold and windy November day. A plant shop sells gardening gifts, pots and plants. Llanarthne, Carmarthenshire SA32 8HG. Open most days. Tel 01558 668768, www.gardenofwales.org.uk

Malus 'Evereste'

One of the merits of this small tree, being self-fertile and very floriferous, is that it is perfect for even a small garden. In the spring, dark pink buds unfold to pure white blooms with a sweet apple blossom scent. In turn, this gives rise to an abundance of small, perfectly formed orange-red apples, their surface streaked with scarlet striations. Cut branches make excellent indoor floral decoration and the fruits make a rich amber crab apple jelly. What better gift for the winter table – if you have the time.

HEIGHT/SPREAD Depends on rootstock. Commonly MM106 gives 3-4m x 3m. AGM.
ORIGINS Hybrid of garden origin.
CONDITIONS Most fertile garden loams.
SEASON Flowers May to June, with fruits September to December. **CM**

Cercidiphyllum japonicum

The light pyramidal profile of this tree gives scope for mixed woodland planting underneath. While *Cercidiphyllum* has rather dull flowers in spring, distractions of *Helleborus* and *Pulmonaria* work their magic. In autumn, shortening days and colder nights advance autumnal colouring and observers are treated to leaves of luminous golden yellow. A chemical reaction within the leaf structure exudes a delicious smell of caramelised sugar.

HEIGHT/SPREAD 15-20m x 8-12m. AGM.
ORIGINS From southern Japan, Sichuan and western China.
CONDITIONS Deep, fertile soil, planted in a sheltered position.
SEASON Glorious foliage from October to November. Spring frosts can damage new foliage, but a second flush of leaves should ensue. **CM**

"*Young leaves are flushed bronze in spring, maturing through green to a beautiful rose madder in the autumn. When leaves finally fall, dense clusters of lilac and purple fruits are thrown into glorious prominence*"

Callicarpa bodinieri var. *giraldii* 'Profusion'

Callicarpa bodinieri var. giraldii 'Profusion'

As a child I would buy aniseed pearls, which glowed the same iridescent purple as these berries. I can quite see why passing birds find them irresistible. Young leaves are flushed bronze in spring, maturing through green to a beautiful rose madder in the autumn. When leaves finally fall, dense clusters of lilac and purple fruits are thrown into glorious prominence. This is a self-fertile variety, which can be relied upon for plentiful fruiting display without the need for multiple specimens.

HEIGHT/SPREAD **2.5m x 2m over a long time.** AGM.
ORIGINS **Widespread from east to west China.**
CONDITIONS **Most fertile loams from acidic to lightly alkaline.**
SEASON **Flowers July-August, fruits October-December. CM**

Lunaria annua

This is a plant with twin peaks. Early spring flowers of rosy purple give rise to papery 'moon-like' seeds, which in winter command attention throughout the borders. At first, outer seed husks appear a rather dingy flat beige, but patience is rewarded, and as the seeds ripen, the outer faces fall away to reveal a perfect white surface with pearl-like luminosity. Impatient gardeners may assist the process by gently rubbing between forefinger and thumb. Be sure to let some seeds fall to perpetuate the display for next year.

HEIGHT/SPREAD 60cm x 30cm.
ORIGINS Central and southern Europe.
CONDITIONS Any fertile garden loam.
SEASON Flowers in May, seeds from November to December. **CM**

DAVE PORTER / ALAMY

Fagus sylvatica

Each winter I am struck by the delicious dark caramel colour of this foliage as it glows in shafts of wintery sunshine. *Fagus sylvatica*, common beech, is so versatile a gardener need be constrained only by imagination and space. Whether clipped hedge, topiaried forms, or as full-grown trees, the species punctuate the landscape with rich tones that offer welcome contrast to the greys and greens of winter. Invest in a bundle of hedging plants and start your own family topiary series for 2025.

HEIGHT/SPREAD Often limited by cultural intervention. AGM.
ORIGINS Europe, eastwards to Ukraine. Southern Scandinavia.
CONDITIONS Well-drained fertile soil from alkaline to mildly acidic. Dislikes waterlogging.
SEASON New foliage in April, autumn colours from October to December. **CM**

JASON INGRAM

Hydrangea quercifolia Snowflake (= 'Brido')

It is the giant oak-like leaves of this plant that draw comment at this end of the year, turning to gregarious shades of russet, burgundy and red. The arching clusters of triangular-shaped flowers, which appear first in July as creamy white, fade to a pretty pinkish hue by September. By December they have transformed into senesced golden cones – perfect for Christmas. Protect from drought and shelter from prevailing winds.

HEIGHT/SPREAD 2m x 2m, though somewhat lax in habit.
ORIGINS Species native to south-eastern United States of America.
CONDITIONS Humus-rich, moisture-retentive soil, neutral to acidic.
SEASON Flowers July to September, good foliage colour until December. **CM**

JASON INGRAM

Places to visit

Chris Marchant names some of her favourite gardens and other places to see plants at their best.

Waddesdon Plant Centre, situated in the old kitchen gardens of Waddesdon Manor, has a particular sparkle at this time of year. Their discerning buyer ensures December ranges include a variety of indoor floral displays: forced bulbs, scented *Narcissus* 'Paper White' and flamboyant amarylis to light up a gloomy corner. Decking the house for

Waddesdon Manor, Christmas display

WWW.WADDESDON.ORG.UK

winter celebrations offers a pleasant distraction from freezing outdoor temperatures. Every year the Christmas decorations at Waddesdon have a different theme. If you get chilled, the Plant Centre café offers fresh coffee and home-made cakes. The Plant Centre is in the grounds at Waddesdon Manor or accessed via Queen Street, Waddesdon. Plant

Cornus alba 'Sibirica'

Many shrubs have coloured stems but none is as easy to grow nor as dramatic as dogwood. *Cornus alba* 'Sibirica' has crimson stems that glow even on dull winter days; when the sun catches them they are dazzling. They look best planted in large groups, either by themselves or with groups of other dogwoods. *Cornus sericea* 'Flaviramea' (in the background of this picture) has olive-yellow stems and *Cornus alba* 'Kesselringii' has dark purple ones. The three of them planted close by each other create a magnificent picture.

HEIGHT/SPREAD 1.5m x 50cm. AGM.
ORIGINS From Eastern Europe to the Baltic, Russia, Mongolia and China.
CONDITIONS Full sun or dappled shade.
SEASON November to March. **JH**

Cotoneaster frigidus 'Cornubia'

Believed to be a hybrid of two diploid species: *Cotoneaster frigidus* from the Himalayas and *C. salicifolia* from central China. The hybrid has occurred more than once, giving rise to several different forms, but 'Cornubia' makes a very elegant, pendulous small tree with an abundance of vibrant red fruits through the autumn into winter. The effect is a welcome rush of colour in the last months of the year. Its diminutive stature makes it eminently suitable for smaller urban gardens which demand high return on invested space.

HEIGHT/SPREAD 5-8m x 3-5m. AGM.
ORIGINS Hybrid from North Indian and Chinese origin.
CONDITIONS Well-drained garden loam.
SEASON Flowers in May, fruits from October to December. **CM**

Vinca difformis

Coming from warmer climates, this *Vinca* is marginally less hardy than other species, but to my mind its grace and extensive flowering period make it worth the small risk. Arching stems erupt from a central clump, bearing unusually large five-petalled flowers in shades of French powder blue that command attention. The floral display peaks in spring and autumn, though a smattering of flowers continues intermittently most of the year. An enduring under-storey to woodland plantings, it requires only an annual trim in February to maintain an orderly habit.

HEIGHT/SPREAD 35cm x 35cm. AGM.
ORIGINS North Africa and south-west Europe.
CONDITIONS Any fertile garden loam.
SEASON April to May and October to December. **CM**

centre open most days. Tel 01296 658586, www. waddesdon.org.uk/shop-and-eat/plant-centre

Now is the time to start thinking about festive food for Christmas celebrations. Visit **local Christmas farmers' markets** for an opportunity to celebrate all that is good about home-grown produce for the table: regional cheeses, cured meats and smoked fish; local wines and piquant relishes. Markets are great for picking up festive essentials while soaking up the seasonal atmosphere. These tempting displays remind us that cold weather does at least bring on a hearty appetite. Check the website www.localfoods.org.uk for the market nearest to you.

Mistletoe is a parasite and can only grow on tree branches. Its favourite host is apple, where it can grow prolifically. The town of Tenbury Wells, at the centre of Worcestershire's apple orchards, hosts Britain's biggest mistletoe auction, the centrepiece of an annual **Mistletoe Festival** held from late November until Christmas. www.tenbury-mistletoe-festival.co.uk

Ludlow Christmas market

Chimonanthus praecox 'Grandiflorus'

Wintersweet is well named as its waxy flowers perfume the cold air through the depths of winter. In China, this lax shrub grows to about 4m in open woodland, but in England it needs a warm position in full sun to ripen wood in preparation for flowering. Traditionally, it is grown against a south or west-facing wall and pruned back to a framework immediately after flowering. 'Grandiflorus' is the largest flowered form and a picked sprig will perfume the whole room.

HEIGHT/SPREAD **4m x 3m.** AGM.

ORIGINS **Native to China, found on the cliffs and in glens and gorges.**

CONDITIONS **Likes fertile, well-drained soil.**

SEASON **Large, deep yellow flowers, with maroon centres, appear through late winter. DP**

Viburnum tinus 'Eve Price'

In the search for unusual and exotic plants it is easy to become blind to the qualities of common-or-garden cultivars. *Viburnum tinus* is a ubiquitous shrub because it is tough, easy-to-grow and attractive. It needs no mollycoddling nor any special conditions to thrive. The leathery, dark green foliage is the perfect foil to the flat clusters of dusky pink buds and the white, starry, scented flowers. In the autumn it produces bunches of metallic-blue berries. I've seen it tightly clipped in columns, alternating with beech to make a striking formal hedge.
HEIGHT/SPREAD Eventually 2m x 2m. AGM.
ORIGINS This is a cultivar of a Mediterranean species.
CONDITIONS Well-drained soil.
SEASON Flowers December to March with berries in the autumn. **JH**

Helleborus x *ericsmithii* 'Winter Sunshine'

H. x *ericsmithii* has distinguished origins. Firstly, botanist Frederick Stern crossed *H. lividus* with *H. argutifolius* to produce the robust and attractive *H.* x *sternii*. Sixty years ago plantsman Eric Smith crossed this with the large white flowers of *H. niger*. The result was a jewel of a plant with lightly marbled foliage and pink-tinged, white flowers. Thanks to micro-propagation, attractive forms of this plant can be reproduced easily. This one is vigorous and has dark green leaves with a pewter sheen. The flowers are ivory-white, turning deep pink as they age.
HEIGHT/SPREAD 40cm x 35cm.
ORIGINS Garden hybrid.
CONDITIONS Rich, well-drained soil in part-shade.
SEASON December to March. **JH**

"Wintersweet is well named as its waxy flowers perfume the cold air through the depths of winter. A sprig picked for the house will perfume the whole room"

Chimonanthus praecox 'Grandiflorus'

Cyclamen coum
Pewter Group

A position under the dappled canopy of deciduous trees allows light to feed this winter-flowering species and keep them on the dry side while they are dormant in the summer. Flowers in shades of magenta persist for several months over leaves that have been selected for their predominance of silver colouring, although a dark green midrib highlights this tone. Happiest without competition, it is nonetheless good company for snowdrops.

HEIGHT/SPREAD 10cm x 15cm. AGM.

ORIGINS Cyclamen coum is native to the mountains of Turkey, the Caucasus region and northern Iran.

CONDITIONS Humus-rich, but prefers dry ground in its dormant period in summer.

SEASON Flowers January to March. **DP**

Clematis cirrhosa var. purpurascens 'Freckles'

This *Clematis* cultivar has a first flush of blooms in November, but continues flowering in all the winter months. Turn the pendant cream blooms upside down to reveal the maroon speckling within. It is vigorous and completely evergreen in a warm spot and, although it likes a sunny wall, it will be happy, though less floriferous, in shade. Fluffy, silky seedheads in autumn; leaves tinged bronze in winter; pale, silver-grey fruits in the summer.

HEIGHT/SPREAD 3-4m x 1.8m. AGM.

ORIGINS The species is a native of southern Europe and the Mediterranean, including the Balearic islands.

CONDITIONS Moist but well-drained soil.

SEASON All year interest. **DP**

Arum italicum 'Marmoratum'

It would be difficult to imagine the winter garden without the spear-shaped, marbled foliage of this form of lords and ladies. Happy in deep shade or in the open, it is in leaf throughout the dormant season. This is perfect as a foil for other winter flowers, but cut the orange truncheon of seed before it fully ripens, or you will have them everywhere. Note that this can also be found named as 'Pictum'.

HEIGHT/SPREAD 30cm x 30cm. AGM.

ORIGINS Arums can be found in southern Europe, North Africa and West Asia to the western Himalayas.

CONDITIONS Likes well-drained, humus-rich soil.

SEASON Pale green and yellow flowers in the summer with orange and red fruits in autumn. **DP**

Places to visit

John Hoyland names some of his favourite gardens and other places to see plants at their best

Winter is a time for walking through woods and admiring landscapes. **The National Pinetum at Bedgebury** close to the Kent/East Sussex border is home to the world's most comprehensive collection of conifers. In all there are 1,800 species of trees and shrubs from five continents, set among 300 acres of land. It is a magical place to stroll

National Pinetum, Bedgebury

around, especially on bright, crisp winter days. The trees are given the space to grow as they would have in the wild, and the planting schemes underline just how beautiful conifers can be. Even a short avenue of mature *Leylandii* looks breathtaking. Bedgebury Road, Goudhurst, near Cranbrook, Kent TN17 2SJ. Open most days.

Hamamelis x *intermedia* 'Jelena'

If I had to restrict myself to one witch hazel, this would be it. Although the *H.* x *intermedia* crosses are not as highly scented as *H. mollis*, the warm colouring of 'Jelena' in autumn and winter more than compensates. A wide plant, branching to 3m and as much across, 'Jelena' is one of the earliest to start flowering, even at Christmas in a mild year. Although *Hamamelis* prefer cool, acid conditions, it can tolerate lime if the soil is deep and rich in humus.
HEIGHT/SPREAD 3m x 3m. AGM.
ORIGINS East Asia, North America.
CONDITIONS Moist and humus-rich, but well-drained.
SEASON Copper flowers in winter; leaves orange-red and yellow in autumn. **DP**

SARAH CUTTLE

Ilex aquifolium 'JC van Tol'

A self-fertile female with no need for a mate, you can guarantee berries on your 'JC van Tol' throughout the winter, making this English holly a very popular source of food with the birds. With foliage that glimmers in the winter sunshine, the lustrous, dark green leaves are less prickly than most hollies and held on dusky purple stems. This can be trimmed to make an impressive hedge, too.
HEIGHT/SPREAD 6m x 4m. AGM.
ORIGINS Europe and West Asia.
CONDITIONS Tolerant of most soil types, fertile and moist, but well drained.
SEASON Bright red berries through winter; tiny white flowers in the spring. **DP**

ANDREA JONES

Chaenomeles x *superba* 'Lemon and Lime'

Easily grown as a low, fairly compact shrub or trained up a wall where space is tight, this winter-flowering quince is aptly named. Cool and clean, it makes a fine contrast to its candy-coloured cousins. The lime green in the flowers complements the previous year's fruits, which hang on empty branches. The shrub is happy in shade although it is heavier flowering when grown in sun.
HEIGHT/SPREAD 1.5m x 2m.
ORIGINS Mountain woodland in Japan and China.
CONDITIONS Light, well-drained soil.
IN SEASON Flowers from February to April; the large fruits are ochre-coloured in the winter. **DP**

HEATHER EDWARDS/GAP PHOTOS

Tel 01580 879820, www. forestry.gov.uk/bedgebury **Studley Royal and Fountains Abbey** covers 800 acres in North Yorkshire and is a Unesco World Heritage Site. The 18th-century canals, lakes and temples are surrounded by woodlands and a deer park, so there's plenty of space to get away from the crowds and enjoy a quiet winter walk. The ruins of the 12th century abbey are especially atmospheric. It is not a place you can rush around, so allow plenty of time for your visit. Ripon, near Harrogate, North Yorkshire HG4 3DY. Seasonal opening. Tel 01765 608888, www. fountainsabbey.org.uk

In Fife, the **Cambo Estate** is best known for its snowdrops, but even before they flower the 70 acres of

NADIA ISAKOVA / ALAMY

Fountains Abbey

beech, oak, sycamore and ash are beautiful. The woodland garden is full of the scent of winter-flowering shrubs. Follow the path along the burn through oak, beech and ash woods to reach the sea. Cambo House, Kingsbarns, St Andrews, Fife KY16 8QD. Open most days. Tel 01333 450054, www.camboestate.com

Rosa 'Nevada'

Nevada in Spanish means snow-clad. How appropriate then, for this overtly generous flowering creamy-white rose, a *rugosa* hybrid, was raised in Spain in 1927 and is presumably named after the Sierra Nevada Mountains. A virtually thornless shrub standing taller than a man, the first avalanche of large, semi-double flowers cascades over the branches in May. Flamboyant as opposed to perfectly fashioned, each flower has a boss of pollen-decked, golden stamens and a sweet, intense, *rugosa*-like scent. Being recurrent, there will be a bud for a buttonhole for months.

HEIGHT/SPREAD 2.2m x 2.2m. AGM.
ORIGINS First bred in Spain.
CONDITIONS Likes fertile and moist but free-draining soil.
SEASON Flowers May to first frosts. **GG**

TORIE CHUGG

SHARON PEARSON

Chionochloa rubra

I am constantly poking fun at what seem to be dead brown grasses. Mostly they aren't grasses at all but sedges, members of the *Cyperaceae* family from New Zealand. *C. rubra* actually is a dead-looking grass, yet it's one of my top 30 plants. In the depths of winter (or in the middle of a cold spring) it graces the nursery and makes me smile. The colour is a glossy brown (if it was really dead it would be a limp straw colour). The shape is a graceful fountain. It moves in the wind and shimmers in sunlight. Fabulous.

HEIGHT/SPREAD 1m x 1.5m.
ORIGINS *Caryopteris* grows wild in the Himalayas and western Asia.
CONDITIONS Light, moist and well drained.
SEASON Flowers late summer and early autumn. **BB**

SHARON PEARSON

"Slender, silvery buds, silky as a cat's ear, stud the stems, a jewel-like spectre, glistening on sunny days throughout winter before bursting to offer up spring flowers"

Salix acutifolia 'Blue Streak'

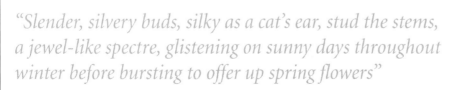

Sanguisorba 'Cangshan Cranberry'

This was collected in a wet meadow in China by planthunter Dan Hinkley in 1996. Selling this burnet under its collection number DJHC 535 proved arduous for we nurserymen – until the more tempting name 'Cangshan Cranberry' was conjured by Dan's pal, Marina Christopher. The hovering swarm of upwardly mobile burrs crown equally upright 2m stems which, without recourse to staking and partnered with tawny Helenium and purple Miscanthus, bring the Sanguisorba season to a colourful October climax. This aerial performance persists on a subtler level long into winter as seen here. A peerless plant.

HEIGHT/SPREAD 2m x 1-1.5m.

ORIGINS Yunnan Province, China.

CONDITIONS Moisture retentive.

SEASON Flowers from September to November, followed by seedheads in winter. **GG**

Hedera helix 'Cavendishii Latina'

Ivy is barely appreciated on its home turf. The rest of the world spends lots of money trying to grow what it calls 'English ivy'. It can be destructive: I've seen it fallen off the front of a cottage, complete with the rendering. But it has colourful, shapely evergreen foliage, grows in terrible places (like dry shade) and is a climber requiring no support. You'll appreciate it most if you grow the non-climbing, shrubby kinds created by rooting cuttings of top growth. 'Cavendishii Latina' is a darling.

HEIGHT/SPREAD 1m x 1m.

ORIGINS Europe.

CONDITIONS A tough plant that will tolerate even dry shade.

SEASON All year, but the November flowers are particularly good. **BB**

TORIE CHUGG

RACHEL WARNE

Hamamelis x intermedia 'Arnold Promise'

This witch hazel makes a magnificent shrub that is more compact and less unruly than some *Hamamelis*. The narrow, twisting petals form spidery flowers with a strong, sweet scent; they look fragile but are tough enough to withstand the iciest weather. This *Hamamelis* can also put up with a windy location but it dislikes shallow, chalky soil. Waterlogged conditions will kill it, so it is always worth digging grit into the soil when you plant it.

HEIGHT/SPREAD Eventually 3m x 3m. AGM.

ORIGINS A hybrid of two Asian species; this cultivar bred at Arnold Arboretum, USA.

CONDITIONS Well-drained soil in full sun or dappled shade.

SEASON December to March. **JH**

Salix acutifolia 'Blue Streak'

The refined, lance-shaped, glossy leaves of this violet willow make for a superior plant. Like a good striptease, the dénouement is tantalisingly slow arriving: at last, autumn winds whisk the leaves from the whippy purple branches, unveiling the sinuous shape beneath. Slender, silvery buds, silky as a cat's ear, stud the stems, glistening on sunny days through winter before bursting to offer up spring flowers. Chalky-bloomed stems radiate on bright, dry spring days, another plus for this graceful small tree.

HEIGHT/SPREAD 10m x 12m (if left unpruned). AGM.

ORIGINS *Salix acutifolia* grows wild in Russia and east Asia.

CONDITIONS Fertile soil; likes damp or wet.

SEASON Stems in winter, followed by spring catkins. **GG**

SHARON PEARSON

Places to visit

John Hoyland names some of his favourite gardens and other places to see plants at their best.

Bluebell Arboretum and Nursery in Leicestershire is a great place to visit at any time of the year. Few other nurseries have so many treasures for sale in one place. Surrounding the nursery are six acres of arboretum planted as a living catalogue for the plants they stock. At this time of year, look out for the hazels, witch hazels and daphnes. Annwell

RICHARD BLOOM / GAP PHOTOS

Bluebell Arboretum

Lane, Smisby, Ashby de la Zouch, Leicestershire LE65 2TA. Seasonal opening. Tel 01530 413700, www.bluebellnursery.com

With many trees now devoid of leaves, November encourages better appreciation of ornamental tree barks and silhouettes. The **Sir Harold Hillier Gardens** incorporates a magnificent arboretum with

Galanthus elwesii var. *monostictus* Hiemalis Group

Snowdrops are effective and cheering. Ones that have better foliage, bigger flowers or start early are worth seeking out. This one extends the season at the beginning (when there are fewer attractions) by starting to bloom in November (sometimes October or December). The blooms last until the rest of your snowdrops start to open. It's a toughie, so will survive almost anywhere if it can get some winter sun. I plant it by the path among (dormant) agapanthus.

HEIGHT/SPREAD 12cm x 15cm from a single bulb after three to five years. AGM.

ORIGINS Turkey.

CONDITIONS Heavier soils seem to suit them better than light sandy ones.

SEASON November to January. **BB**

SHARON PEARSON

Ilex x *koehneana*

The chestnut-leaved holly is an airy yet robust conical evergreen tree with wide-spreading branches and leaves that are among the largest and broadest of any holly. As with most hollies *Ilex* x *koehneana* is dioecious, carrying male and female flowers on separate trees. The white flowers are small, opening May to June with females later developing dramatic bunches of tightly packed orange-red berries. By October, trees can be laden with thick clusters of fruit.

HEIGHT/SPREAD 5m x 4m.

ORIGINS A hybrid of the far eastern *Ilex latifolia* and the European *Ilex aquifolium*.

CONDITIONS Sun to part shade in well-drained but moist soil.

SEASON All year round for foliage. October to March for berries. **FG**

TORIE CHUGG

Narcissus romieuxii 'Julia Jane'

Plant these bulbs where you can get to within smelling distance of the flowers. A pot stood on a low wall would do. It is a nice, quietly coloured, early (and the earliness is encouraging) wonderfully scented daffodil with neat, dark green foliage. The perfume is strong but not brash, combining musk and fresh fruit. You'll come back to it time and time again. Any form of *Narcissus romieuxii* is good but this is superlative.

HEIGHT/SPREAD 15cm x 12cm.

ORIGINS Morocco.

CONDITIONS Pots and planters, left outside in full sun or partial shade. Use gritty compost with more grit or pebbles on top to protect flowers from soil-splash.

SEASON Late November to February. **BB**

TORIE CHUGG

comprehensive labelling of mature and young specimens. The Winter Garden, close to the Visitor Pavilion, contains over 650 different plants selected for their seasonal winter effect. There are also tea rooms, a shop, and space for exhibition events throughout the year. Sir Harold Hillier Gardens, Jermyns Lane, Ampfield, Romsey, Hants SO51 0QA. Open most days.

Tel 01794 369317, www3. hants.gov.uk/hilliergardens

The medieval manor house of **Dartington Hall** was given a new lease of life by the American philanthropists Leonard and Dorothy Elmhurst who employed a succession of designers to enhance the garden's potential. Nestled against a sheltering combe, the house looks into an ancient tiltyard, where green terraces

JASON INGRAM

Dartington Hall in Devon

frame a perfect lawn. Artfully positioned cedar trees, a procession of Irish yews and a magnificent Henry Moore reclining statue compose the space nearest the house. A triumph of design with 25 acres of gardens. Open most days. Dartington Hall, Totnes, Devon TQ9 6EL. Tel 01803 847058, www.dartingtonhall.com

SUBSCRIPTION ORDER FORM

GIBZP513

Complete the order form and send to: GARDENS ILLUSTRATED, Freepost SEA5894, Sittingbourne, Kent ME9 8DF (You may photocopy this form)

☑ **YES, I would like to subscribe to GARDENS ILLUSTRATED**

PAYMENT OPTION 1 – Direct Debit

☐ **UK DIRECT DEBIT – Just £24 for 12 issues** by annual Direct Debit – **SAVE 50%***. After your first 12 issues your payments will continue at £34.40 every 12 issues, saving 30%. *(Please complete form below)*

Instructions to your Bank/Building Society to pay by Direct Debit

TO: The Manager (Bank/Building Society)

Address

Name(s) of Account Holder(s)

Bank/Building Society account number

Branch sort code

Reference number *(For internal use only)*

Please pay Immediate Media Co Bristol Ltd Debits from the account detailed in this instruction subject to the safeguards assured by the Direct Debit Guarantee. I understand that this instruction may remain with Immediate Media Co Bristol Ltd and, if so, details will be passed electronically to my bank/building society.

Signature(s)   Date   /   /

Originator's identification number   710644

Banks and Building Societies may not accept Direct Debit instructions from some types of account.

PAYMENT OPTION 2 – Credit or Debit card, cheque

For a year's subscription – 12 issues

☐ **UK credit/debit card or cheque** – £36.90 for 12 issues – **SAVE 25%***
☐ **EUROPE credit/debit card or cheque** – £49.97 for 12 issues
☐ **REST OF WORLD credit/debit card or cheque** – £59.97 for 12 issues
☐ I enclose a cheque made payable to Immediate Media Co Bristol Ltd
     for the amount of £ ....
☐ I would like to pay by credit/debit card, please debit my card:
     ☐ Visa   ☐ Mastercard   ☐ Maestro

Card no. ☐☐☐☐ ☐☐☐☐ ☐☐☐☐ ☐☐☐☐ ☐☐☐☐

Expiry date ☐☐/☐☐   Issue no. (Maestro only) ☐☐

Signature ....   Date ....../....../......

YOUR DETAILS (Essential)

Title   Forename

Surname

Address

                         Postcode

Country

Home tel no.

Mobile tel no.**

Email address**

Immediate Media Company Limited (publishers of GARDENS ILLUSTRATED) would love to keep you informed by post or telephone of special offers and promotions from the Immediate Media Company Group. Please tick if you would prefer not to receive these ☐.
** Please enter this information so that GARDENS ILLUSTRATED may keep you informed of newsletters, special offers and other promotions by email or text message. You may unsubscribe from these at any time.

GIFT SUBSCRIPTION (Recipient details)

☐ I would like to give a gift subscription of GARDENS ILLUSTRATED to:

Title   Forename

Surname

Address

                         Postcode

Country

Daytime tel no.

Email address

* SAVE 50% available to UK annual Direct Debit orders only. After your first 12 issues your payments will continue at £34.40 every 12 issues, saving 30%. UK cheque, debit card and credit card orders will save 25%. Your subscription will start with the next available issue. **Offer ends 31 December 2013.**

50% off

Your subscription offer
• 12 issues for £24 saving 50% on the shop price*
• Just £2 per copy
• Never miss an issue with free UK delivery

Gardens Illustrated *

SPECIAL OFFER

CELEBRATE 100 YEARS OF THE CHELSEA FLOWER SHOW

12 issues for £24 *

S ILLUSTRATED

Where to buy your plants

NOTE: several of these nurseries offer online or mail-order services only, or limited visiting times. Please call before visiting.

ASHWOOD NURSERIES

Ashwood holds the National Collection of *Lewisia* and has an excellent range of hardy cyclamens, hellebores, hepaticas, *Anemone pavonina* and auriculas.
Ashwood Lower Lane, Ashwood, Kingswinford, West Midlands DY6 0AE
01384 401996
www.ashwoodnurseries.com

CLAIRE AUSTIN HARDY PLANTS

Claire Austin holds the National Collection of bearded iris and hybrid herbaceous peonies. The nursery offers a good selection of these, as well as hemerocallis and other hardy plants.
White Hopton Farm, Wern Lane, Sarn, Newtown, Powys SY16 4EN
01686 670342
www.claireaustin-hardyplants.co.uk

DAVID AUSTIN ROSES

Think roses, and chances are the name that springs to mind is David Austin. This nursery is well worth a visit, particularly in early summer when the many different ramblers, climbers, modern shrubs and wild species are at their very best.
Bowling Green Lane, Albrighton, Wolverhampton, West Midlands WV7 3HB
01902 376300
www.davidaustinroses.com

Hemerocallis
'Red Precious'

AVON BULBS

This mail-order outlet sells a comprehensive range of interesting and unusual bulbs. Its excellent online catalogue features about 700 plants.
Burnt House Farm, Mid Lambrook, South Petherton, Somerset TA13 5HE
01460 242177
www.avonbulbs.co.uk

AVONDALE NURSERY

This nursery and display garden has extensive collections of geums, eryngiums, heleniums, agapanthus and geraniums.
Mill Hill, Baginton, Coventry CV8 3AG
024 7667 3662
www.avondalenursery.co.uk

BARNSDALE GARDENS

Barnsdale Gardens has many varieties of penstemons and hemerocallis as well as a wide range of other garden plants.
The Avenue, Exton, Oakham, Rutland LE15 8AH
01572 813200
www.barnsdalegardens.co.uk

PETER BEALES ROSES

Peter Beales has one of the largest classic rose collections in the world, with more than 1,100 varieties including shrub, bush, climbing, rambling and ground cover roses.
London Rd, Attleborough, Norwich, Norfolk NR17 1AY
01953 454707
www.classicroses.co.uk

BINNY PLANTS

Specialising in new and unusual perennials, ferns and grasses, Binny Plants has a particularly good range of euphorbias, geraniums, hostas, peonies and iris.
Binny Estate, Ecclesmachan, West Lothian EH52 6NL
01506 858931
www.binnyplants.com

THE BOTANIC NURSERY

This nursery specialises in lime-tolerant plants, including home-grown foxgloves, ferns, grasses, perennials, shrubs and climbers.
Near Stonar School, Atworth, Wiltshire SN12 8NU
07850 328756
www.thebotanicnursery.co.uk

BROADLEIGH BULBS

This nursery is renowned for its small bulbs, including an excellent range of cyclamens, snowdrops, crocuses, tulips and herbaceous plants.
Barr House, Bishops Hull, Taunton, Somerset TA4 1AE
01823 286231
www.broadleighbulbs.co.uk

TOBY BUCKLAND NURSERIES

The renowned plantsman offers a wide range of perennials, annuals, biennials, exotics and bulbs, as well as grasses and shrubs.
The Walled Garden, Powderham Castle, Kenton, Devon EX6 8JQ
01626 891133
www.tobybuckland.com

BURNCOOSE NURSERIES

More than 3,500 ornamental trees, shrubs and herbaceous plants are available at this nursery. Look out for rare and unusual magnolias and rhododendrons.
Gwennap, Redruth, Cornwall TR16 6BJ
01209 860316
www.burncoose.co.uk

CALLY GARDENS

Several thousand varieties of unusual perennials can be seen here, with hundreds for sale in the nursery.
Gatehouse of Fleet, Castle Douglas, Kirkcudbrightshire DG7 2DJ
01557 815029
www.callygardens.co.uk

CATH'S GARDEN PLANTS

This family-run nursery is set within the walls of an old walled garden. It stocks a wide range of herbaceous perennials, as well as a number of more unusual shrubs, grasses, ferns, herbs, wall shrubs and climbers.
Heaves Hotel, Heaves, Nr Levens, Cumbria LA8 8EF
015395 61126
www.cathsgardenplants.co.uk

Viburnum tinus
'Eve Price'

BETH CHATTO GARDENS

Beth Chatto's nursery is what you'd expect from one of the UK's most respected plantswomen. The display garden and nursery offer ideas for planting in difficult areas. More than 2,000 plants are available to buy, with an emphasis on herbaceous perennials and bulbs.
Elmstead Market, Colchester, Essex CO7 7DB
01206 822007
www.bethchatto.co.uk

CLIFTON NURSERIES

Clifton Nurseries offers an excellent range of plants, plus containers, sculpture, furniture, cut flowers and gifts.
5A Clifton Villas, Little Venice, London W9 2PH
020 7289 6851
www.clifton.co.uk

COBLANDS

This online garden centre delivers an array of garden plants, shrubs, herbaceous perennials, grasses, climbers, ferns, bamboos, bulbs and garden tools.
Trench Rd, Tonbridge, Kent TN11 9NG
01732 770999
www.coblands.co.uk

COTSWOLD GARDEN FLOWERS

Founded in 1991 by Bob Brown, Cotswold Garden Flowers is a small nursery specialising in unusual and easy-to-grow hardy herbaceous perennials and smaller shrubs. It holds the National Collection of *Sambucus*.
Sands Lane, Badsey, Evesham, Worcestershire WR11 7EZ
01386 833849 (nursery),
01386 422829 (mail order)
www.cgf.net

CROCUS

This online and mail-order nursery has won plenty of awards. It has a massive range of plants available, as well as gifts and tools.
Nursery Court, London Rd, Windlesham, Surrey GU20 6LQ
0844 557 2233/2244
www.crocus.co.uk

Aronia melanocarpa
'Autumn Magic'

CRÛG FARM PLANTS

Crûg Farm Plants specialises in unusual herbaceous perennials, climbers and shrubs. The nursery holds the National Collections of *Paris*, *Coriaria* and *Polygonatum*.
Griffith's Crossing, nr Caernarfon, Gwynedd LL55 1TU
01248 670232
www.crug-farm.co.uk

DAISY ROOTS

Daisy Roots specialises in healthy, hardy perennial plants and grasses.
8 Gosselin Rd, Bengeo, Hertford, Herts SG14 3LG
01992 582401
www.daisyroots.com

DOVE COTTAGE NURSERY & GARDEN

Enjoying panoramic views of Shibden and Chelsea valleys and a hillside of mixed woodland, this nursery and garden features a wide range of perennials and grasses.
Shibden Hall Rd, Halifax, West Yorkshire HX3 9XA
01422 203553
www.dovecottagenursery.co.uk

DUCHY OF CORNWALL NURSERY

Set in an old slate quarry near Restormel Castle , this nursery sells 4,000 varieties of plants, including trees, shrubs, conifers, roses, perennials, fruit and half-hardy exotics.
Cott Rd, Lostwithiel, Cornwall PL22 0HW
01208 872668
www.duchyofcornwallnursery.co.uk

DYSON'S NURSERIES

William Dyson, curator at Great Comp Garden, runs this nursery specialising in salvias and offering an eclectic range of other choice and uncommon hardy and half-hardy plants.
Comp Lane, Platt, Borough Green, nr Sevenoaks, Kent TN15 8QS
01732 885094
www.greatcompgarden.co.uk/dysonsnurseries.html

EDROM NURSERIES

Woodland plants are in abundance at Edrom, particularly trilliums, arisaemas, primulas and anemones. There is also an excellent range of alpines, bulbous plants, ferns and trees and shrubs.
Coldingham, Eyemouth, Berwickshire TD14 5TZ
01890 771386
www.edrom-nurseries.co.uk

EDULIS

Paul Barney specialises in unusual perennial plants, many of them edible, obtained on plant-hunting forays to exotic locations including India, China and Chile.
1 Flowers Piece, Ashampstead, Reading,
Berkshire RG8 8SG
01635 578113
www.edulis.co.uk

FARMYARD NURSERIES

This nursery offers a range of hellebores and unusual herbaceous plants, tricyrtis and schizostylis, and garden plants including shrubs, trees and alpines.
Llandysul, Carmarthenshire SA44 4RL
01559 363389
www.farmyardnurseries.co.uk

FERNATIX

Steven Fletcher and Kerry Robinson have turned a love of ferns into a thriving nursery and online/mail order business selling hardy ferns, greenhouse species and cultivars.
Stoke Ash, Suffolk IP23 7EN
www.fernatix.co.uk

FIBREX NURSERIES

Fibrex is home to the National Collections of *Pelargonium* and *Hedera*. Set in the heart of the Warwickshire countryside, it specialises in hardy ferns and hellebores, all propagated and grown on site.
Honeybourne Rd, Pebworth, Stratford-upon-Avon, Warwickshire CV37 8XP
01789 720788
www.fibrex.co.uk

Dryopteris expansa
RACHEL WARNE

FOXGROVE

Foxgrove sells a good range of hardy and unusual plants, including galanthus, hellebores, grasses, penstemons and alpines.
Foxgrove, Enborne, Newbury, Berkshire RG14 6RE
01635 40554
www.foxgroveplants.co.uk

Hedera helix 'Cavendish Latina'
TORIE CHUGG

GREAT DIXTER NURSERY

Head gardener Fergus Garrett continues Christopher Lloyd's legacy of bold, innovative planting at Great Dixter. The nursery, which stocks many of the plants grown on site, has a good selection of clematis, shrubs and perennials.
Northiam, Rye, East Sussex TN31 6PH
01797 254044
www.greatdixter.co.uk

HALL FARM

This award-winning nursery grows and propagates a wide range of herbaceous plants, including hardy geranium, grasses, bog plants and pool marginals.
Vicarage Lane, Kinnerley, nr Oswestry, Shropshire SY10 8DH
01691 682135
www.hallfarmnursery.co.uk

HALLS OF HEDDON

This family-run nursery, established in 1921 by William Nicholson Hall, specialises in dahlias and chrysanthemums.
Heddon on the Wall, Newcastle upon Tyne NE15 0JS
01661 852445
www.hallsofheddon.co.uk

HARDY'S COTTAGE GARDEN PLANTS

More than 1,200 herbaceous perennials are available at this family-run plant nursery in Hampshire, plus a good range of hardy geraniums, *Viola odorata* and Parma violets.
Priory Lane Nursery, Freefolk Priors, Whitchurch,
Hampshire RG28 7NJ
01256 896533
www.hardys-plants.co.uk

HARVEYS GARDEN PLANTS

Roger Harvey's nursery is now one of the UK's finest, with a superb collection of hellebores. You'll also find herbaceous perennials and woodland plants.
Great Green, Thurston, Bury St Edmunds, Suffolk IP31 3SJ
01359 233363
www.harveysgardenplants.co.uk

HAYLOFT PLANTS

The selection offered by six keen female gardeners reflects their interest in the origins and history of the plants they sell.
The Pack House, Manor Farm Nurseries, Pensham, Pershore, Worcestershire WR10 3HB
01386 562 999
www.hayloft-plants.co.uk

HOO HOUSE NURSERY

Large range of herbaceous and alpine plants, with display borders and garden holding the National Collection of *Platycodon* and *Gentiana asclepiadea*.
Gloucester Rd, Tewkesbury, Gloucestershire GL20 7DA
01684 293389
www.hoohouse.plus.com

KEVIN HUGHES PLANTS

This specialist nursery at Heale Gardens offers hardy plants including many wisterias, Raymond Evison clematis, trilliums, more than 80 magnolias, lilacs, viburnums and philadelphus, plus shade plants, and those for chalk and dry gardens and for wildlife interest.
Heale Gardens, Middle Woodford, Salisbury, Wiltshire SP4 6NT
01722 782504
www.kevinsplants.co.uk

KEVOCK GARDEN PLANTS

This mail-order online plant centre offers a variety of interesting and unusual plants from all over the world. It is a truly international collection and many of the plants are tested in the owners' garden south of Edinburgh.
16 Kevock Road, Lasswade, Midlothian EH18 1HT
0131 454 0660
www.kevockgarden.co.uk

KNOLL GARDENS

Neil Lucas has established this as one of the best places in the UK to buy grasses. Around two hundred forms of ornamental grasses are available and there is a large display garden to visit. Neil holds the National Collection of *Pennisetum*.
Hampreston, Wimborne, Dorset BH21 7ND
01202 873931
www.knollgardens.co.uk

LONG ACRE PLANTS

This charming nursery specialises in unusual woodland perennials, and stocks an excellent range of bulbs and ferns.
Charlton Musgrove, Somerset BA9 8EX
01963 32802
www.plantsforshade.co.uk

Salvia nemorosa 'Caradonna'
RACHEL WARNE

ELIZABETH MACGREGOR NURSERY

Old and new varieties of violas are the speciality, plus hardy geraniums, penstemons, campanulas, eryngiums, iris and primulas. The herbaceous garden is spectacular in mid summer.
Ellenbank, Tongland Road, Kirkcudbright, Dumfries & Galloway DG6 4UU
01557 330620
www.elizabethmacgregor nursery.co.uk

MARCHANTS HARDY PLANTS

Graham Gough and Lucy Goffin grow unusual herbaceous perennials and choice grasses. Specialities include kniphofias, agapanthus, sedums, miscanthus and molinias.
2 Marchants Cottages, Mill Lane, Laughton, East Sussex BN8 6AJ
01323 811737
www.marchantshardyplants. co.uk

MADRONA NURSERY

Derek Jarman called this the most charming nursery in England. There is an excellent range of unusual trees, shrubs, perennials, ferns and grasses.
Pluckley Rd, Bethersden, Kent TN26 3DD
01233 820100
www.madrona.co.uk

THE MEAD NURSERY

A wide variety of plants is grown on site, and the mature garden is laid out to give ideas on colour and design, with raised alpine beds, herbaceous borders and a sink garden.
Brokerswood, near Westbury, Wiltshire BA13 4EG
01373 859990
www.themeadnursery.co.uk

THE OLD WALLED GARDEN NURSERY

This nursery specialises in rare and unusual plants from all over the world, particularly Australia.
Honeybourne Rd, Pebworth, Stratford-upon-Avon, Warwickshire CV37 8XP
01789 720788
www.oldwalledgarden.com

Kniphofia rooperi
RACEHL WARNE

PAN-GLOBAL PLANTS

Owner Nick Macer takes his list of rare and desirable plants very seriously, and the result is an exciting collection of trees, shrubs, herbaceous perennials, bamboos, exotics, climbers and ferns.
The Walled Garden, Frampton Court, Frampton-on-Severn, Gloucestershire GL2 7EX
01452 741641
www.panglobalplants.com

PHOENIX PERENNIAL PLANTS

This well-known Hampshire nursery, owned and run by plantswoman Marina Christopher, has an excellent line in perennials and grasses. The nursery's plant list is extensive and diverse.
Paice Lane, Medstead, Alton, Hampshire GU34 5PR
01420 560695

Miscanthus sinensis '**Malepartus**'
RACHEL WARNE

PIONEER PLANTS

Pioneer has one of the most eclectic and garden-worthy collections. Only a limited number of the plants are available by mail order.
Baldock Lane, Willian, Letchworth,

Hertfordshire SG6 2AE
01462 675858
www.pioneerplants.com

READS NURSERY

This nursery, recently relocated from Norfolk, is renowned for its rare and unusual fruit trees as well as conservatory plants.
Douglas Farm, Falcon Lane, Ditchingham, Bungay Suffolk NR35 2JG
01986 895555
www.readsnursery.co.uk

RV ROGER

This century-old nursery business provides a range of field-grown fruit trees, including many traditional varieties that are becoming quite rare, and a huge variety of bulbs, roses, shrubs and ornamental trees.
The Nurseries, Malton Rd, Pickering, North Yorkshire YO18 7JW
01751 472226
http://rvroger.co.uk

SAMPFORD SHRUBS

This small nursery grows a range of common and uncommon garden-worthy plants.
Sampford Peverell, Tiverton, Devon EX16 7EN
01884 821164
http://samshrub.co.uk/

SPECIAL PERENNIALS

The range of unusual and heritage perennials on offer includes more than 80 varieties of hemerocallis, plus geums, old and new phlox, many varieties of monardas, achilleas and persicarias. The

nursery holds National Collections of *helenium* cvs and centaurea.
Yew Tree House, Hall Lane, Hankelow, Cheshire CW3 OJB
01270 811443
www.specialperennials.com

SPECIAL PLANTS NURSERY

Derry Watkins' nursery stocks a sensational range of seeds and plants, including hardy, herbaceous and rockery plants, as well as tender perennials for the terrace and conservatory. Derry's one-day courses are also well worth attending.
Greenways Lane, Cold Ashton, Chippenham, Wiltshire SN14 8LA
01225 891686
www.specialplants.net

THORNCROFT CLEMATIS

This family-run nursery specialises in clematis, growing well-known cultivars, new introductions from around the world and evergreen and herbaceous clematis as well as less common species.
The Lings, Reymerston, Norwich, Norfolk NR9 4QG
01953 850407
www.thorncroftclematis. co.uk

TREHANE NURSERY

This charming nursery offers an unrivalled selection of ericaceous plants, particularly camellias and blueberries, as well as azaleas, magnolias and rhododendrons.
Stapehill Rd, Wimborne, Dorset BH21 7ND
01202 873490
www.trehane.co.uk

Dahlia '**Moonfire**'
RACHEL WARNE

WATERPERRY GARDENS

The shop at these famous gardens stocks an extensive range of trees, shrubs, perennials, alpines and fruit, most grown on site. The historic eight-acre gardens have fine herbaceous borders.
Nr Wheatley, Oxfordshire OX33 1JZ
01844 339226
www.waterperrygardens. co.uk

WHITEWATER NURSERY

The nursery has a wide range of plants: perennials, shrubs and trees, bamboos, grasses, alpines and more. It also has a planting plan service.
Hound Green, Hook, Hampshire RG27 8LQ
0118 932 6487
www.whitewaternursery.co.uk

Clematis cirrhosa '**Jingle Bells**'
RACHEL WARNE

WISLEY PLANT CENTRE

The centre sells some 10,000 different plants, including a wide selection of hardy plants, as well as fruit trees, conservatory and houseplants, bulbs and seeds.
RHS Garden Wisley, Woking, Surrey GU23 6QB
01483 211113
www.rhs.org.uk/ wisleyplantcentre

WOOTTENS OF WENHASTON

This nursery specialises in bearded irises, pelargoniums, auriculas, hemerocallis and herbaceous hardy perennials. In late May, the nursery's iris fields are a sight to behold.
Blackheath, Wenhaston, Halesworth, Suffolk IP19 9HD
01502 478258
www.woottensplants.co.uk